Origami

The Japanese Art of Paper Folding

Yukiko Kurosava

Priority Publications

Fifth Reprint 2016

ISBN 978 81 8022 066 1

Published by Priority Publications
info@dspublishers.com
www.dspublishers.com

Cover Designed by White Mice Media

Printed in India at EIH Ltd. (Unit : Printing Press)
An Oberoi Group Company

Follow the instructions carefully before you start paper folding.

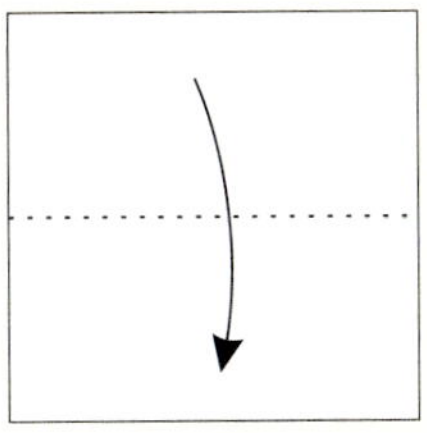

Fold in front....

.... like this.

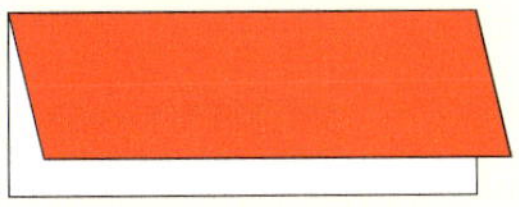

Valley fold (a series of dashes)

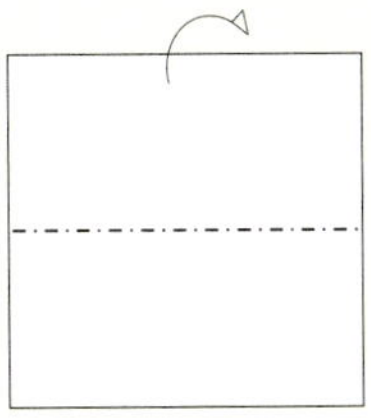

Fold behind....

.... like this.

Mountain Fold (a series of dashes and dots)

Stair-step Fold

This fold is made by combining a Valley Fold and a Mountain Fold to form a kind of pleat or stair-step....

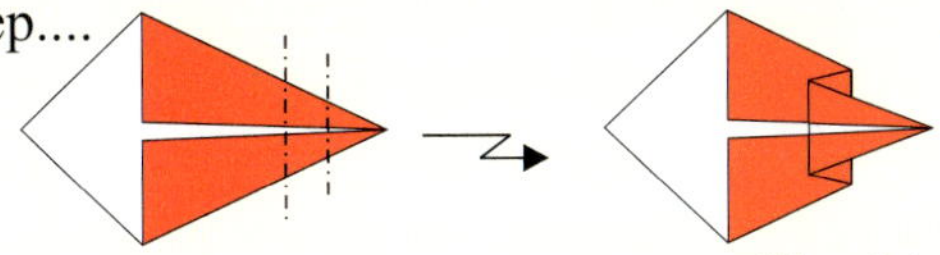

.... like this.

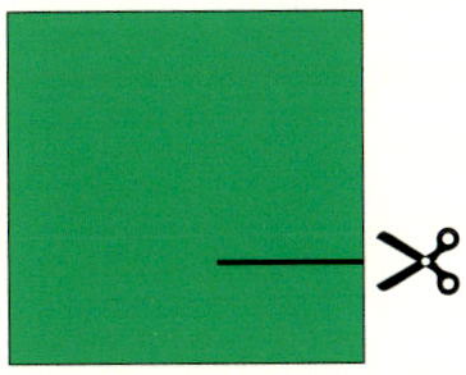

Cut

.... like this.

Fold over and over (like a flattened roll)....

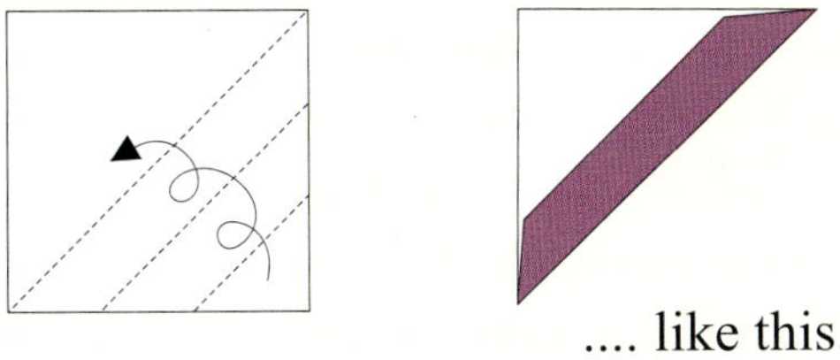

.... like this.

Enlarge

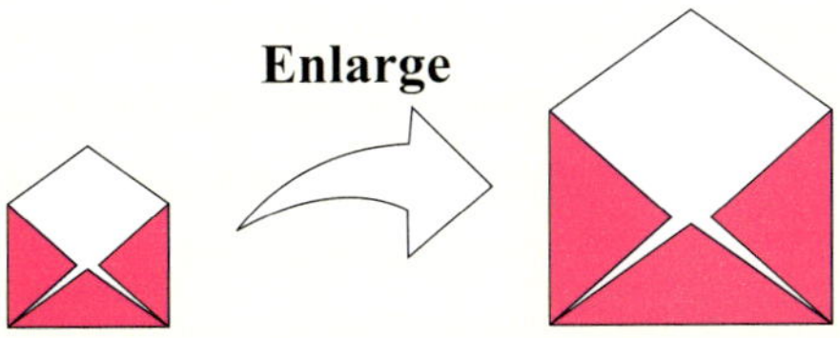

A swollen arrow indicates that next diagram is enlarged.

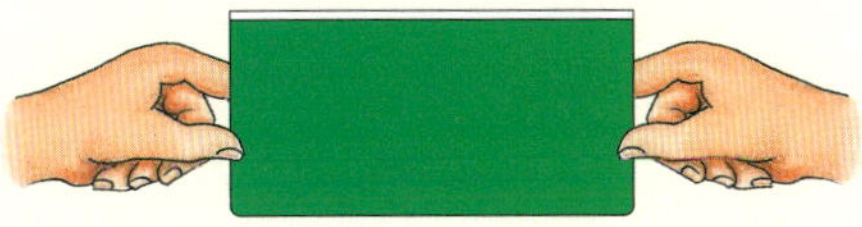

Neatly bring the corners together to coincide exactly.

Turn the model over.... .... like this.

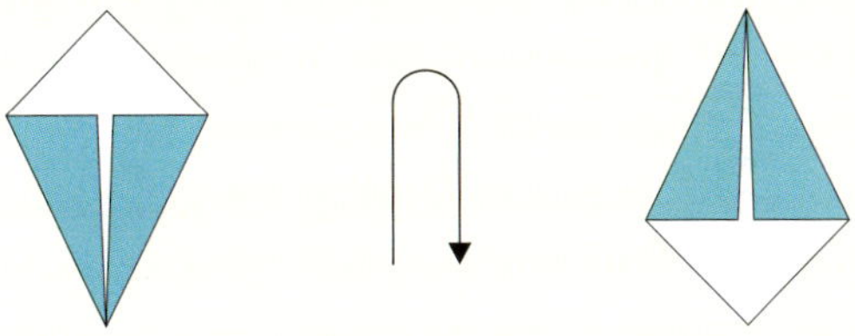

Turn upside down...... .... like this.

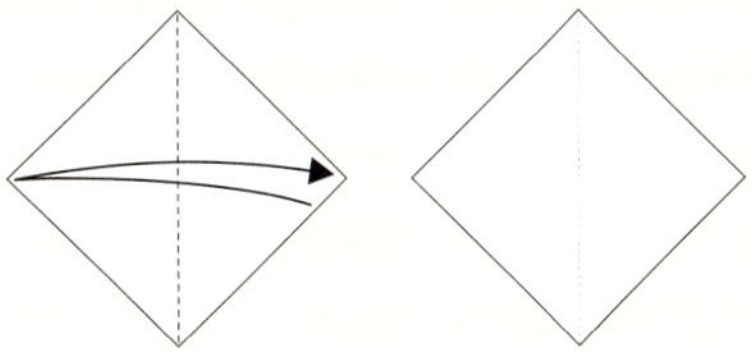

Fold and unfold to make a crease .... like this.

A faint line represents an existing crease line, or one which is the result of a previous step.

Inflate

This "Puff" arrow shows you where to blow.

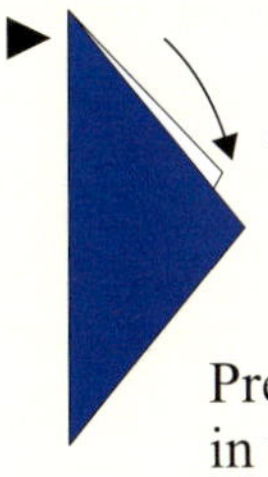

Apply force

Press or push in the required direction.

To sharpen the crease, use the finger-nail and the thumb-nail as shown in the diagram.

Learn to make good Squash Fold, Pocket Fold and Hood Fold.

Squash Fold

1

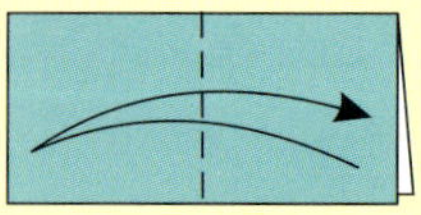

Fold in half and unfold.

2

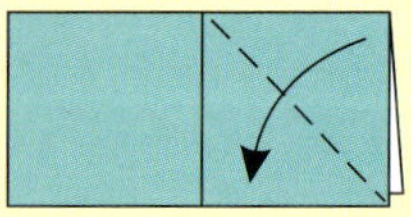

Fold the top right corner forward and backward and then unfold.

3

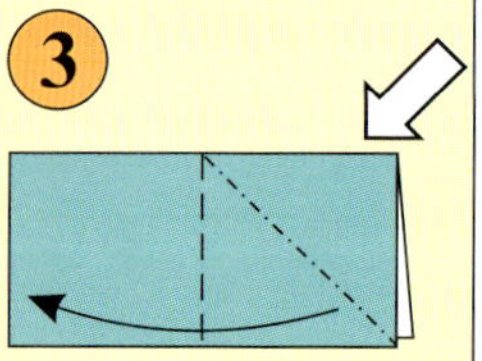

Press the top right corner at its upper edge....

4

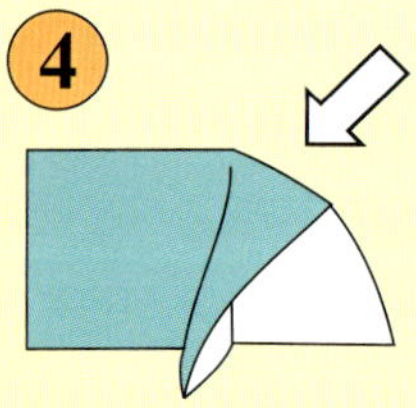

.... to open out into a triangle when flattened....

5

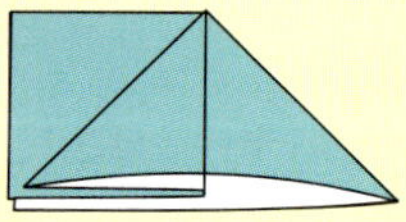

.... like this.

This is a **Squash Fold**.

Pocket Fold

1

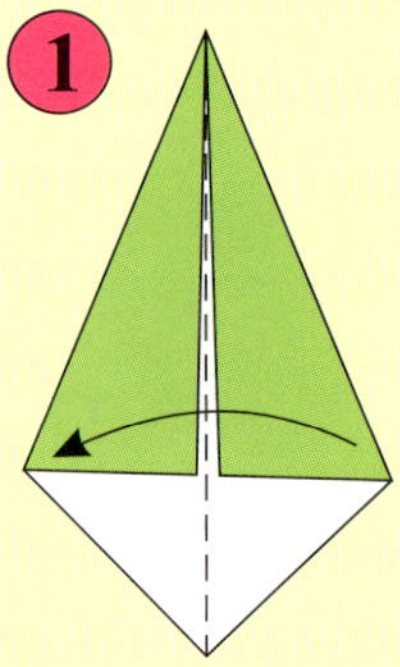

Fold in half from right to left.

2

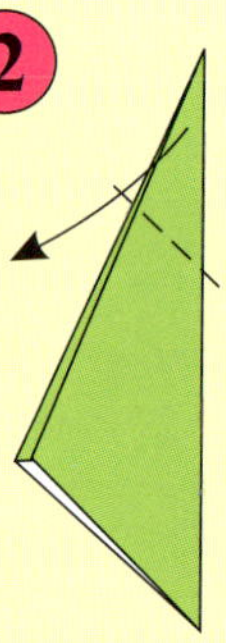

Fold the top corner forward and backward and unfold it.

3

Now fold the top corner at the crease to bring it down between the two layers of the paper....

4

.... reversing its middle crease....

5

… like this.

This is a **Pocket Fold**.

Hood Fold

1

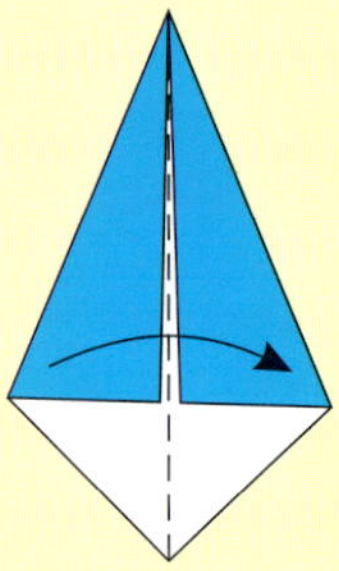

Fold in half from left to right.

2

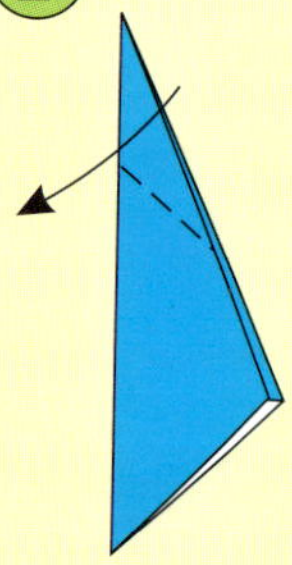

Fold the top corner forward and backward and unfold.

3

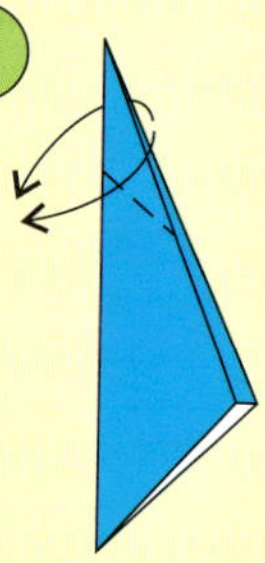

Now, fold the top corner at the crease inside out by slightly opening the flaps....

4

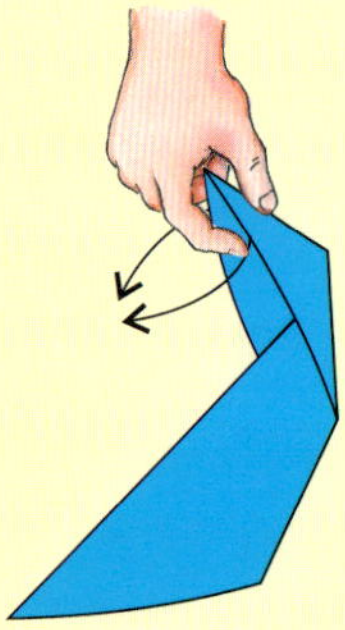

....like this.

5

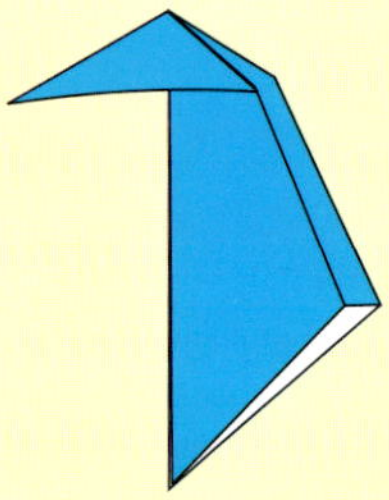

This is a **Hood Fold**.

Contents

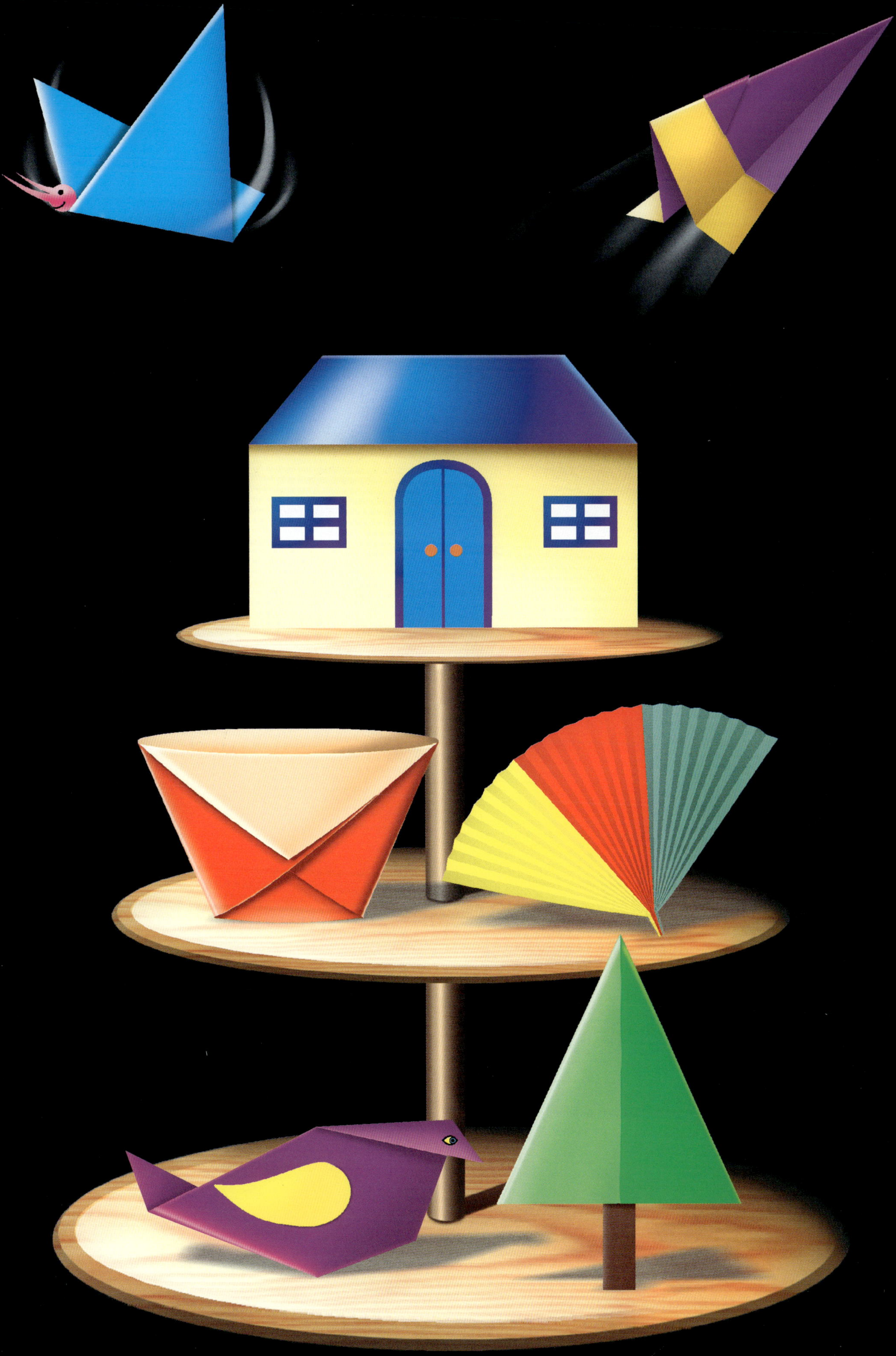

Tree

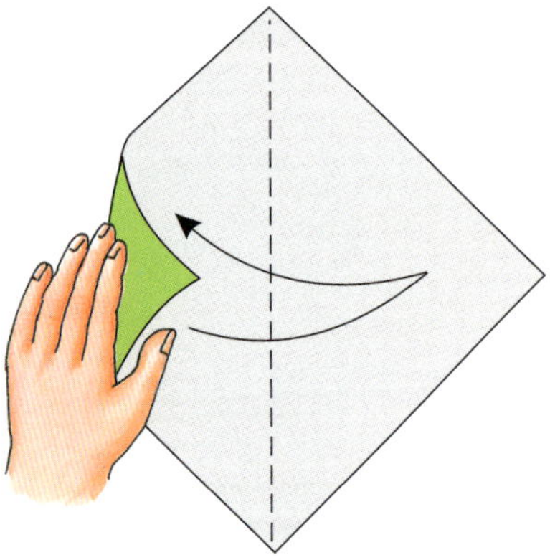

1 Fold along the dotted line to make a centre crease and then unfold it.

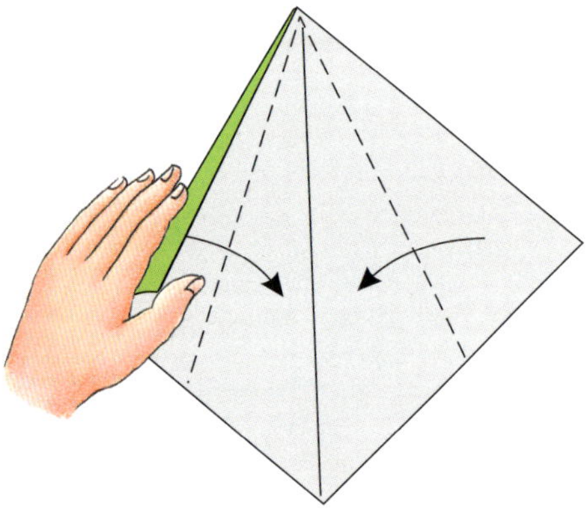

2 Fold the right and left corners to touch the centre line.

3 Now fold the lower end upward along the dotted line and paste it.

4 Paste a brown paper piece to make the trunk of the tree.

5 Now, the tree is ready.

Bird

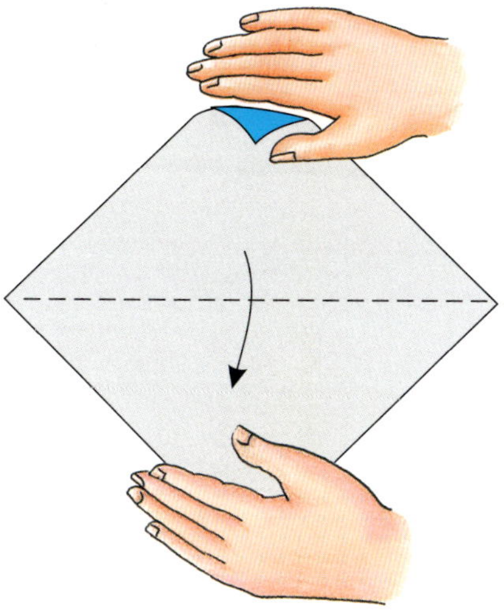

1 Make a centre crease and fold along the dotted line.

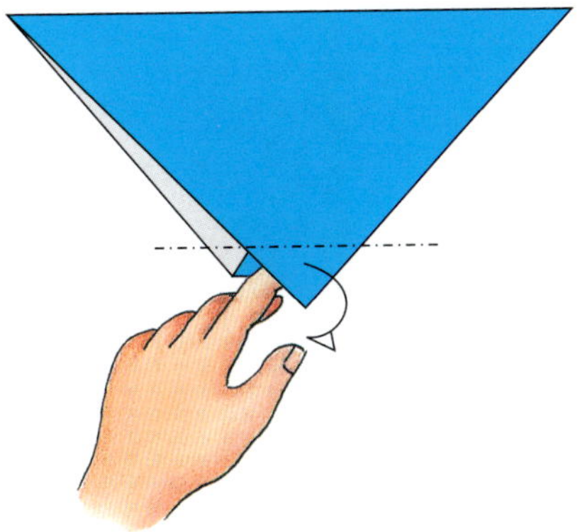

2 Fold the lower part of both the layers inward along the dotted line.

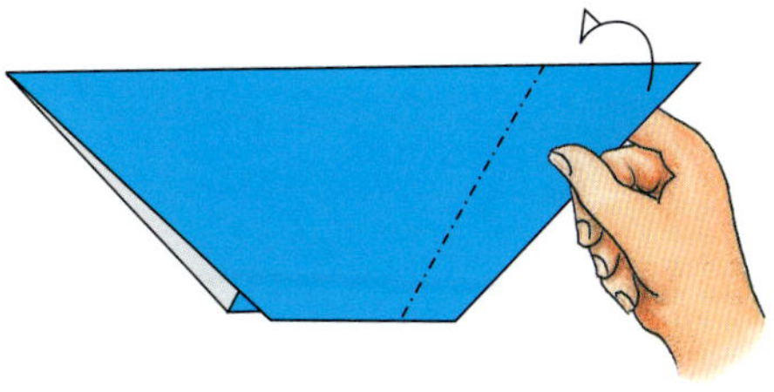

3 Fold the right edge backward along the dotted line.

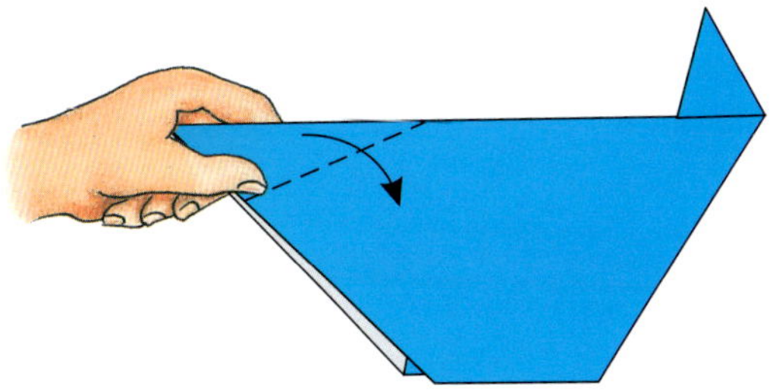

4 Fold the left corner forward as shown along the dotted line.

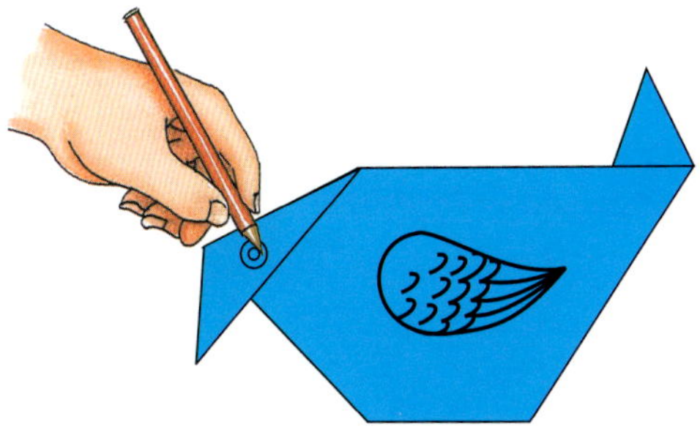

5 Draw an eye and a wing ..... like this.

Butterfly

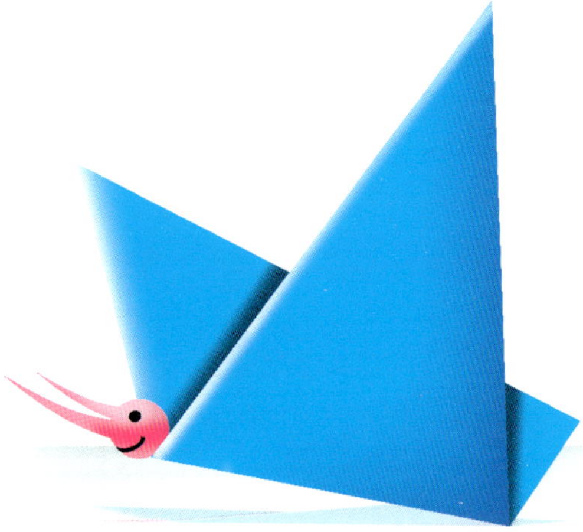

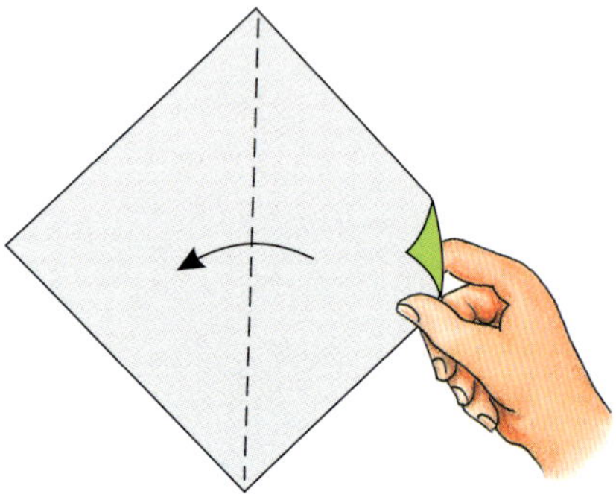

1 Fold along the dotted line.

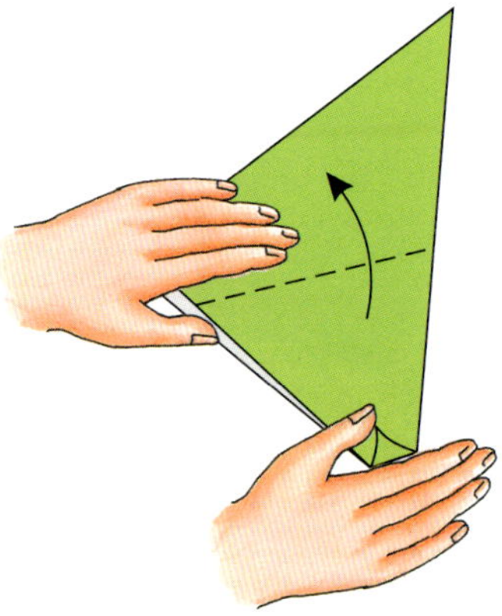

2 Fold the lower flap upward along the dotted line.....

3 ..... like this.

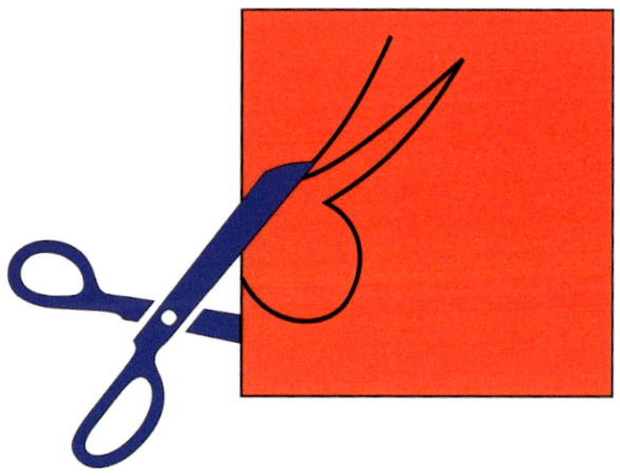

4 Cut a shape of the head from a different coloured paper.

5 Now paste the head on it and draw eye and lips as shown.

Cup

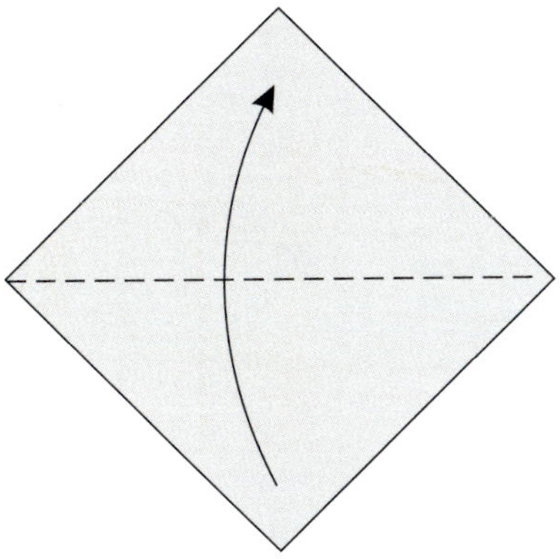

1 Fold along the dotted line in the direction of arrow.

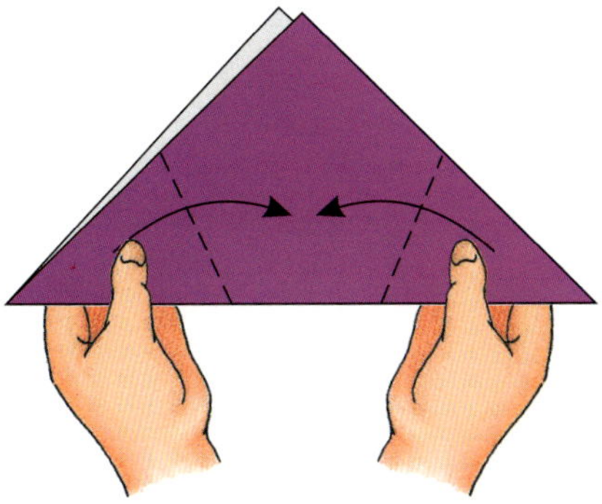

2 Fold the left and right corners to overlap each other.....

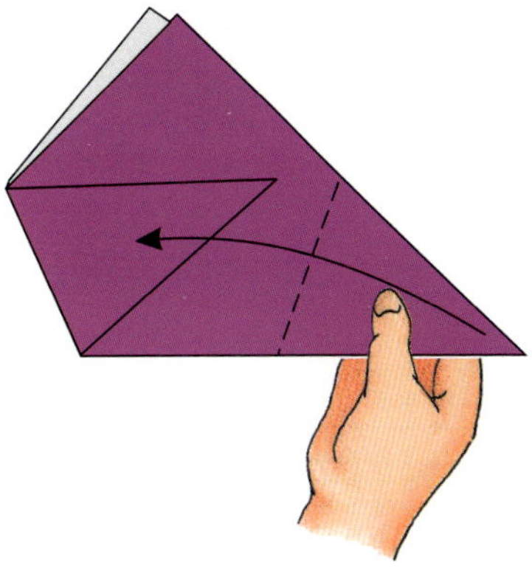

3 ..... like this.

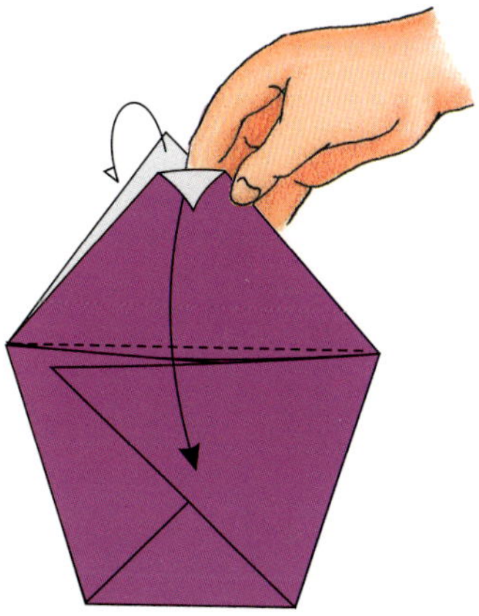

4 Fold the front top layer and back top layer downwards.

5 Now, your cup is ready.

Fan

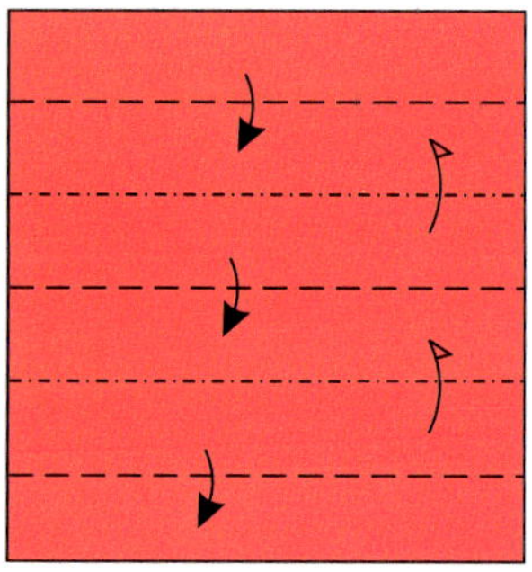

1 Fold 'Valley' and 'Mountain' folds alternately along the dotted lines.....

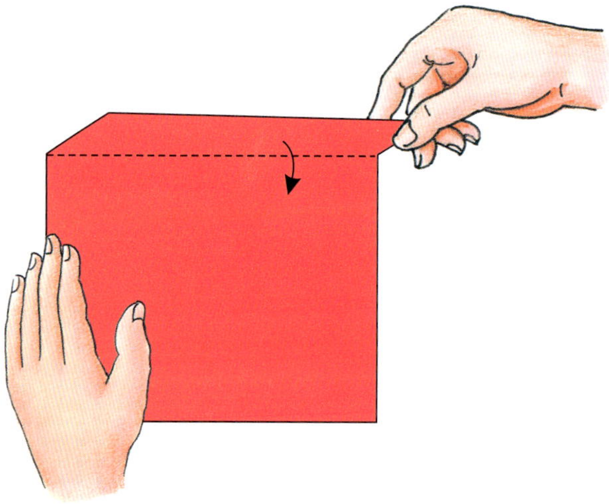

2 ..... in this way.....

3 ..... like this.

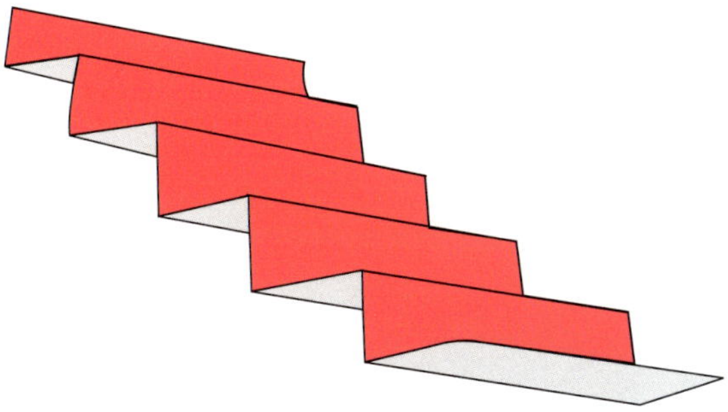

4 Take two different coloured papers and make them fold in this way.

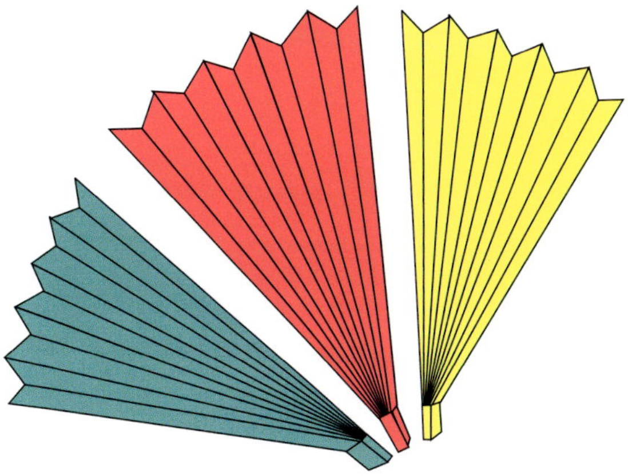

5 Paste them side by side.

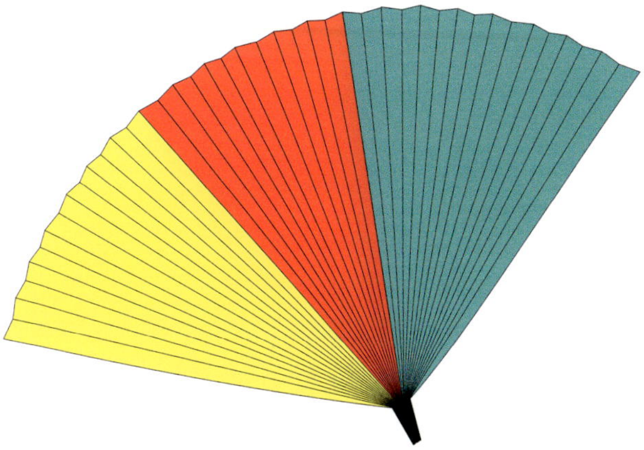

6 Now, your fan is ready.

Home

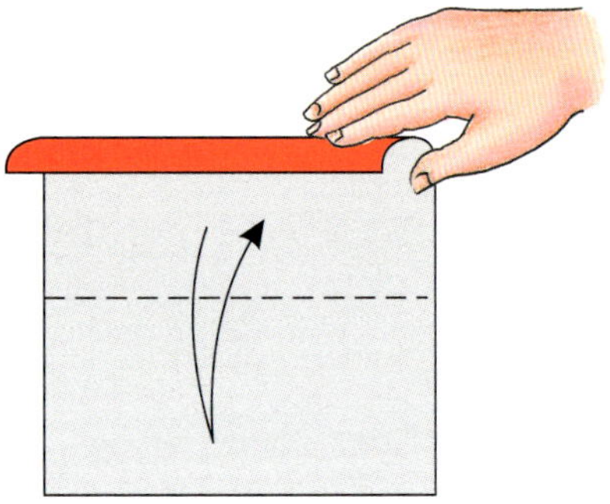

1 Fold and unfold along the dotted line to make a centre crease.

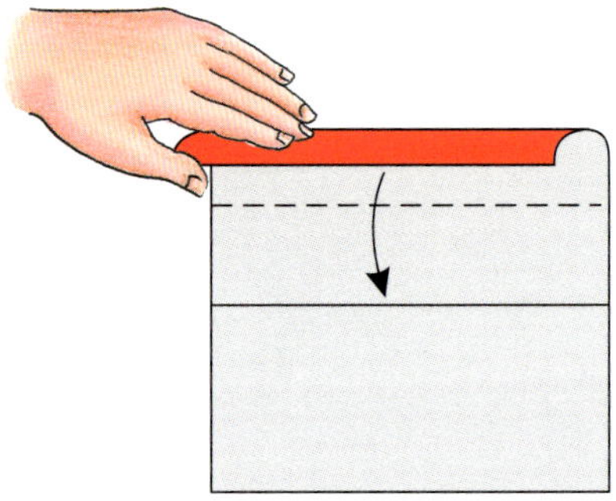

2 Fold the top edge down to the centre crease.

3 Fold the two corners behind along the dotted lines....

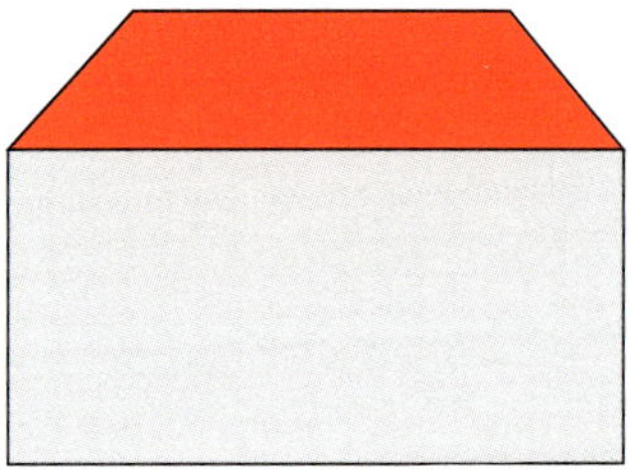

4 .... like this.

5 Draw a door and windows, and your home is ready.

Aeroplane

1 Use ¾th of the paper you have. Make the centre crease and unfold it.

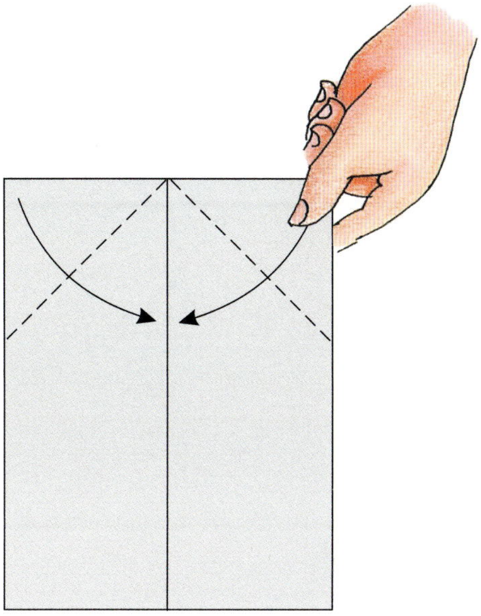

2 Fold both the upper corners to the centre along the dotted lines.

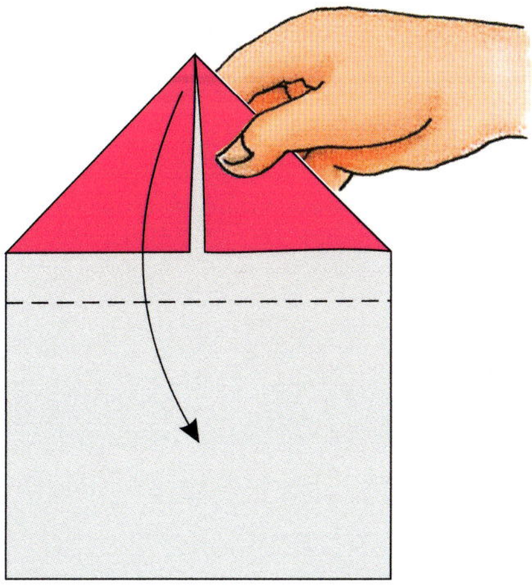

3 Fold the upper part downwards along the dotted line.

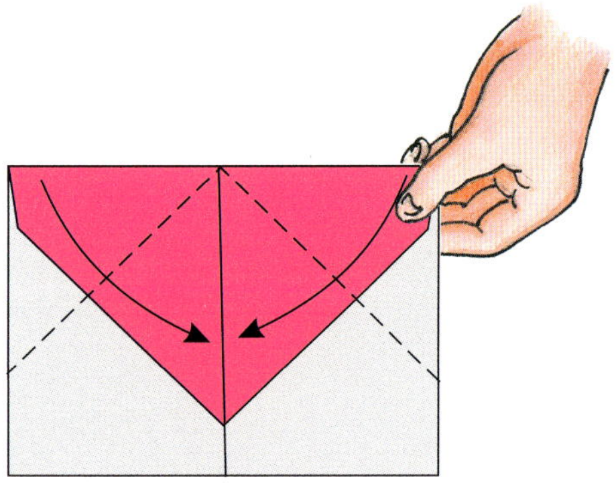

4 Fold both the upper corners to the middle line.

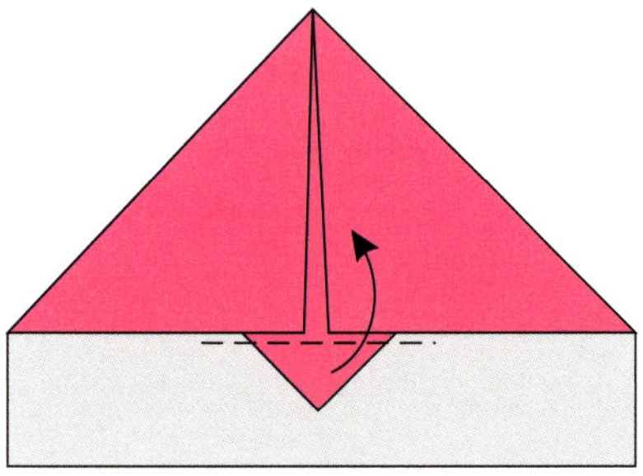

5 Fold the small triangle upwards.

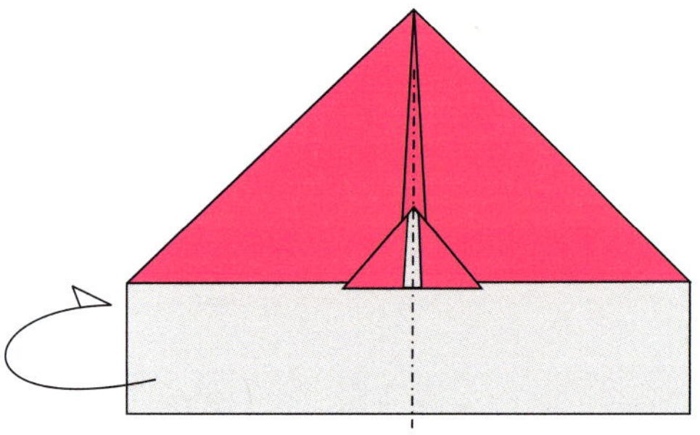

6 Fold the model backwards in half.

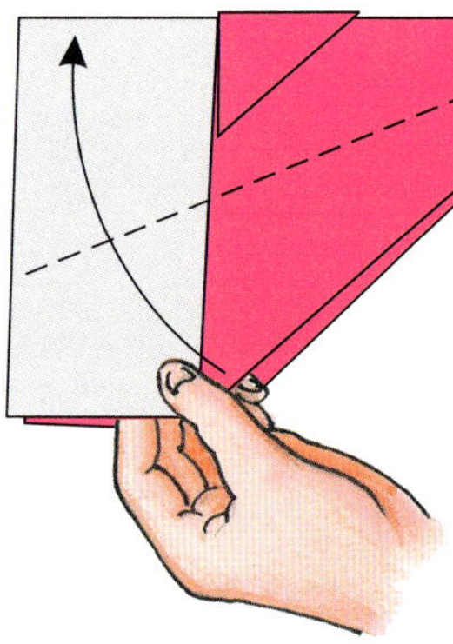

7 Fold the front flap upwards along the dotted line.

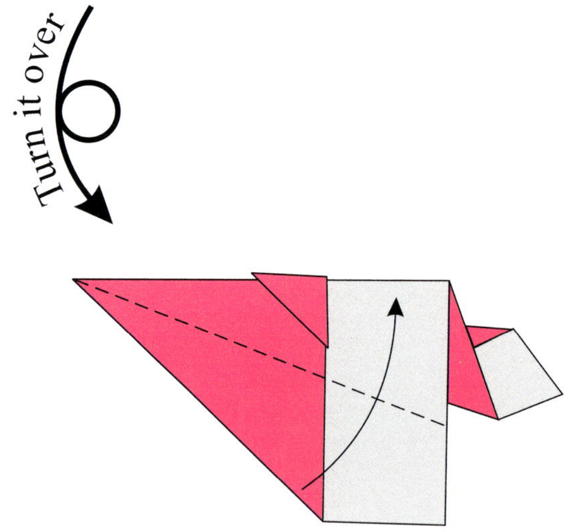

8 Fold the other flap in the same way.

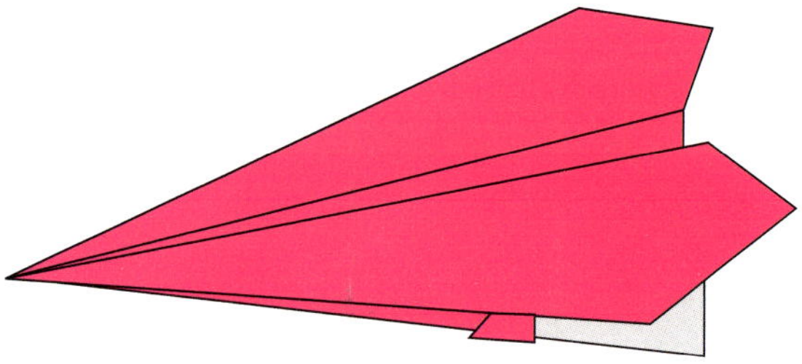

9 Throw this aeroplane up and watch it glide through the air.

Collage Work

Tree

TIPS AND TRICKS

Step-1 Collect paper sheets of various colours of your own choice. Tear them in small pieces of different shapes.

Step-2 Set them within the outline and paste in the given shape.

Cut and Paste

Home

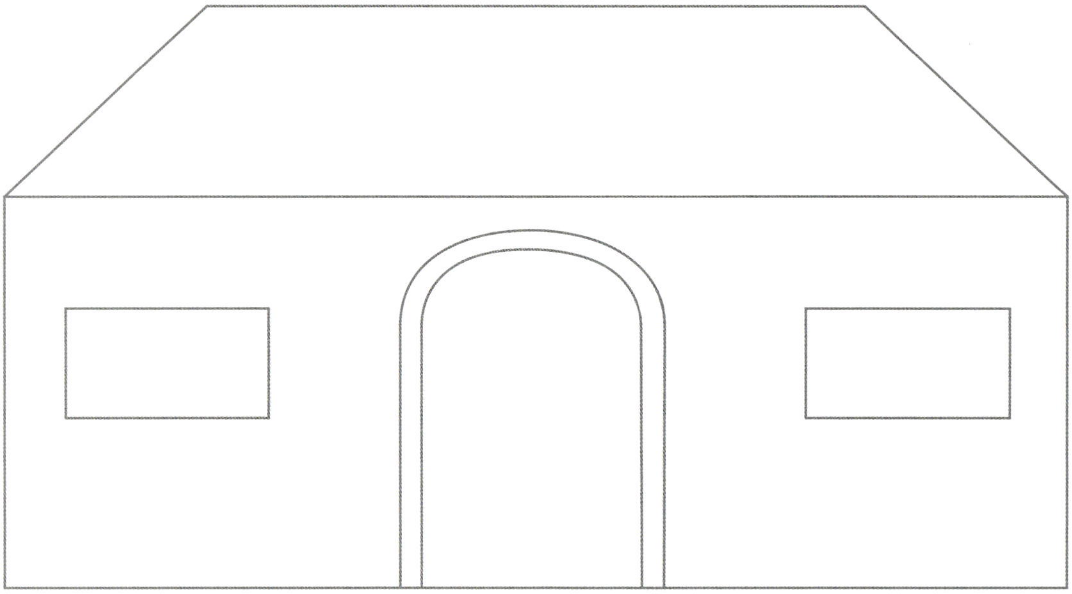

TIPS AND TRICKS

Step-1 Take craft paper sheets of various colours. Trace different parts on the shape of different colours.

Step-2 Now paste these pieces at the appropriate places.

Crushed Paper Art

Cup

TIPS AND TRICKS

Step-1 Take a plain paper and squeeze it in your hand. Open it gently and apply the poster colour with a flat brush.

Step-2 Now cut the paper according to the shape and paste it within the outline.

Spray Paint

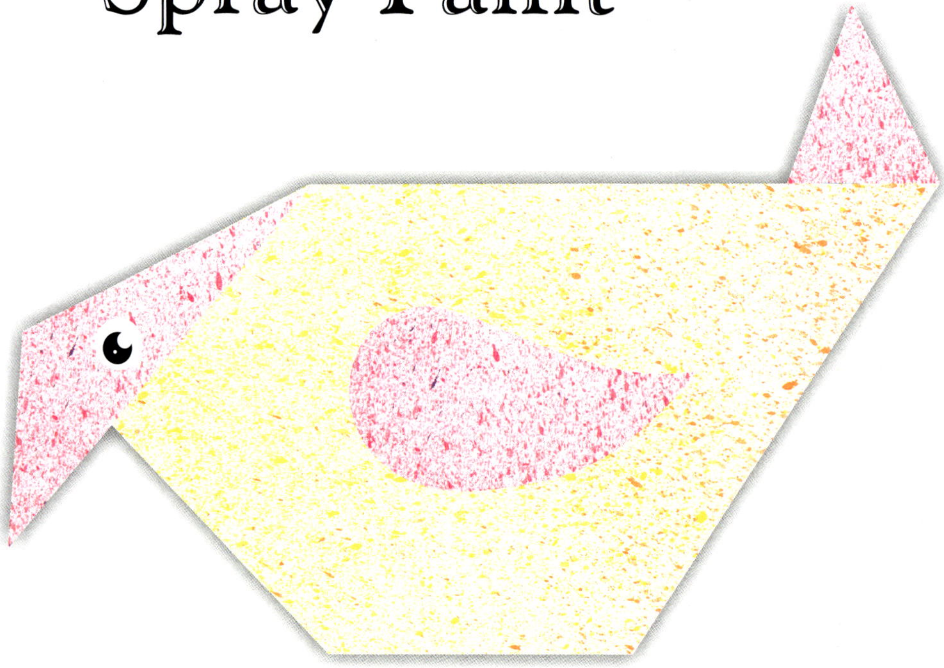

Bird

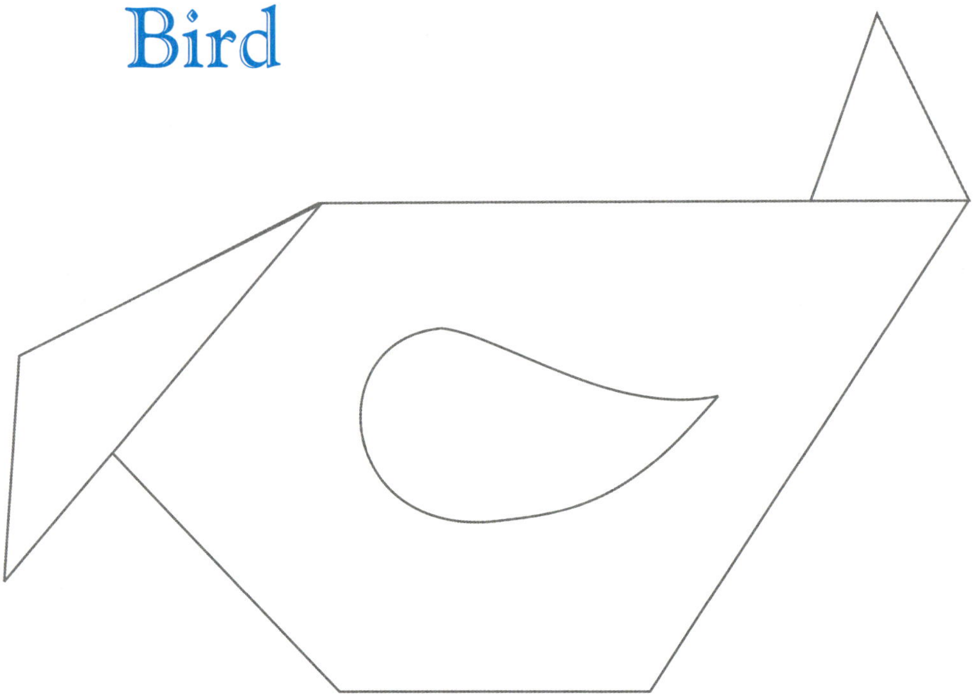

TIPS AND TRICKS

Step-1 Take a white paper. Spray different colours of your own choice with a tooth brush on the white paper.

Step-2 Cut the parts of the shape as per your liking and paste them on the figure.

RESERVE BANK OF INDIA
50

Purse

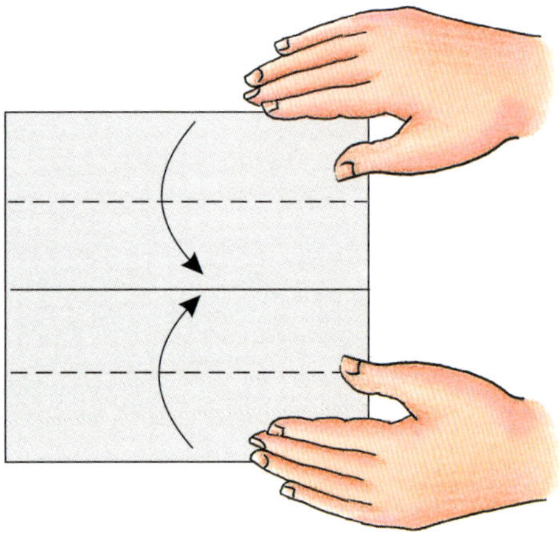

1 Draw lines to divide the paper in four quarters and fold the upper and lower edges along the dotted lines as shown....

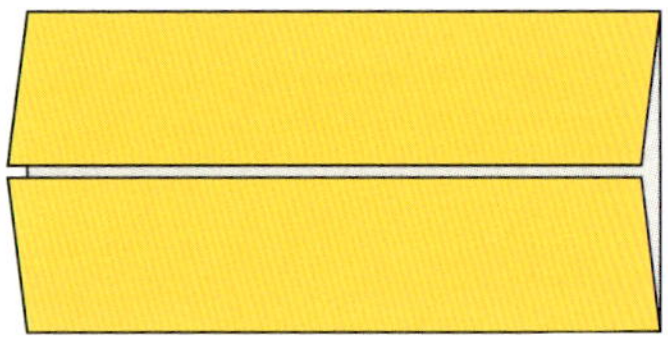

2 ....like this.

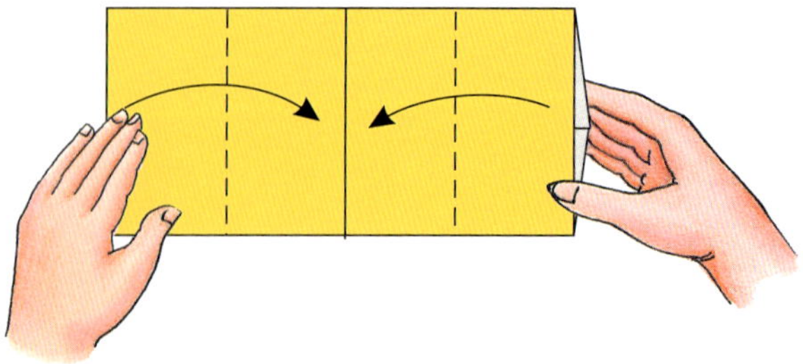

3 Fold both the sides to meet at the centre line.

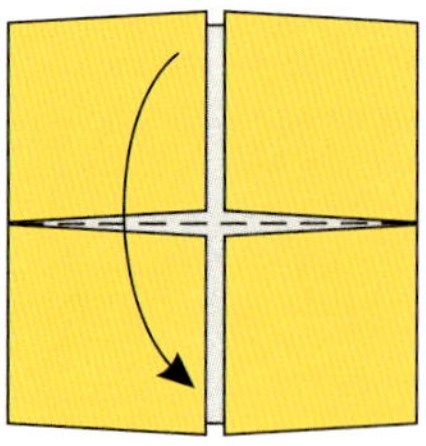

4 Fold in half inward along the dotted line as shown.

5 Finally, draw and decorate it.

Joker

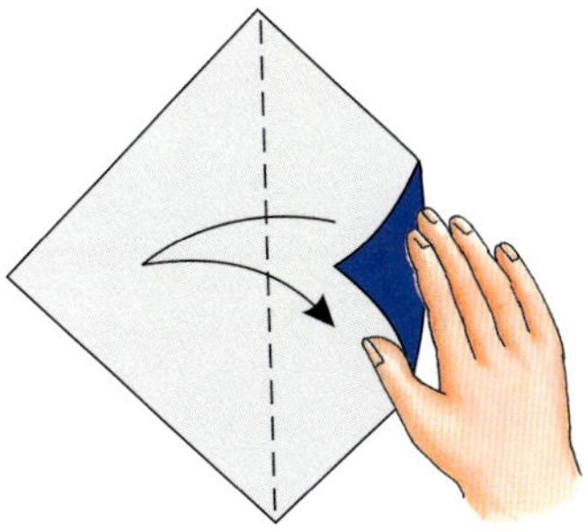

1 Make fold and then unfold as shown.

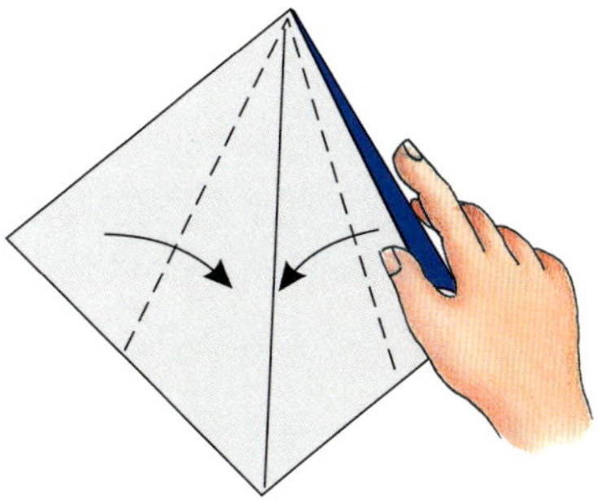

2 Fold both the right and left edges to the centre line....

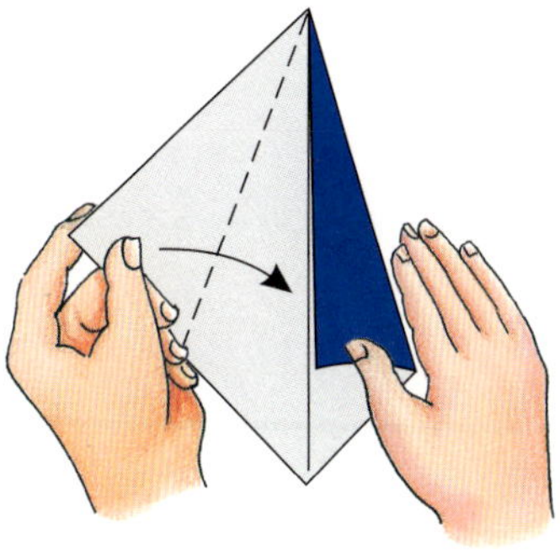

3 .... in this way.

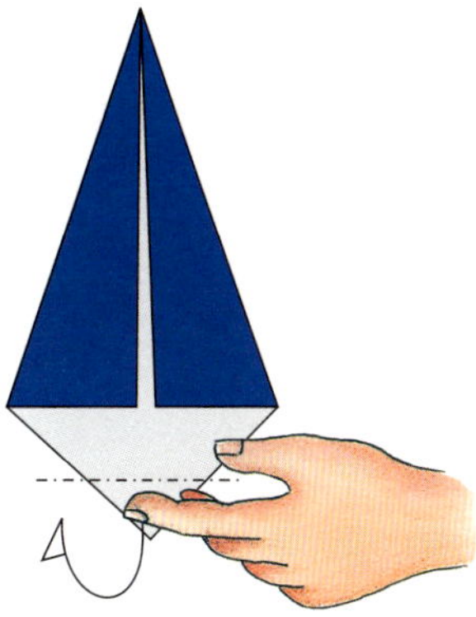

4 Fold the lower part backward along the dotted line.

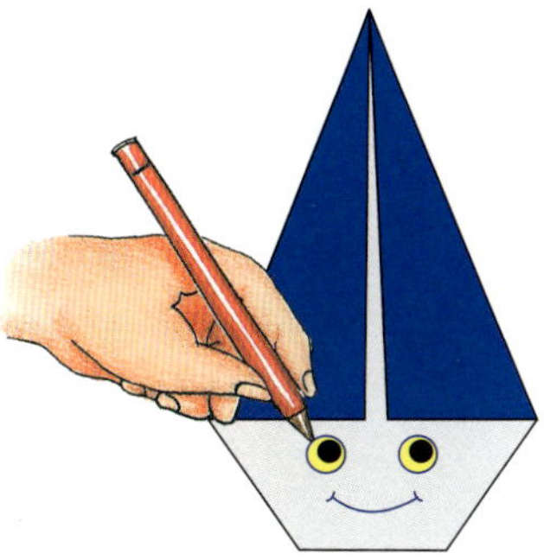

5 Draw the face and hair. Your joker is ready.

Peacock

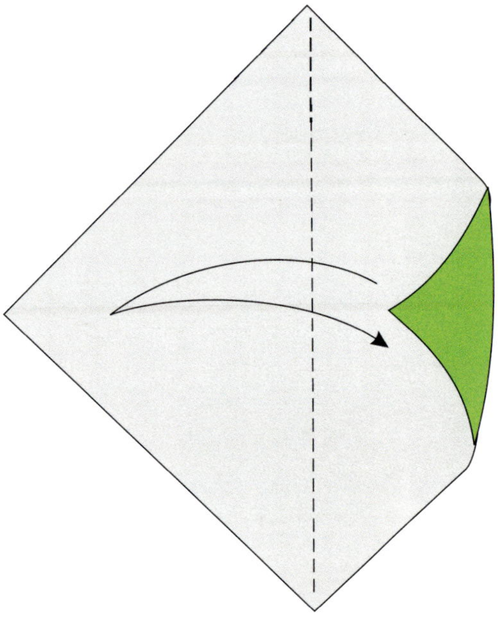

1 Fold to make a centre crease and then unfold.

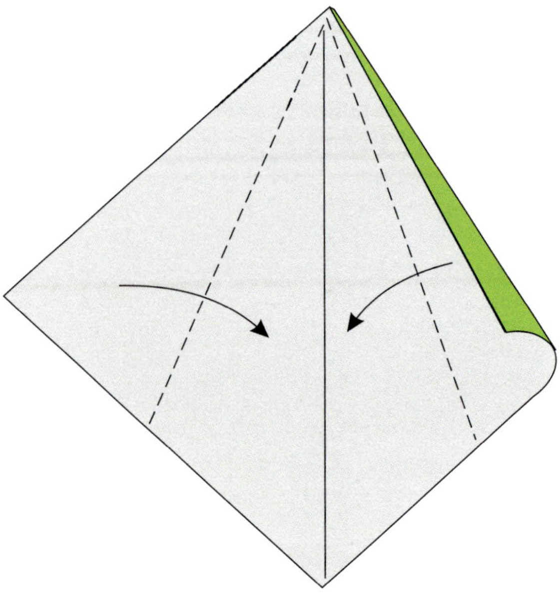

2 Fold the right and left corners to the centre line.

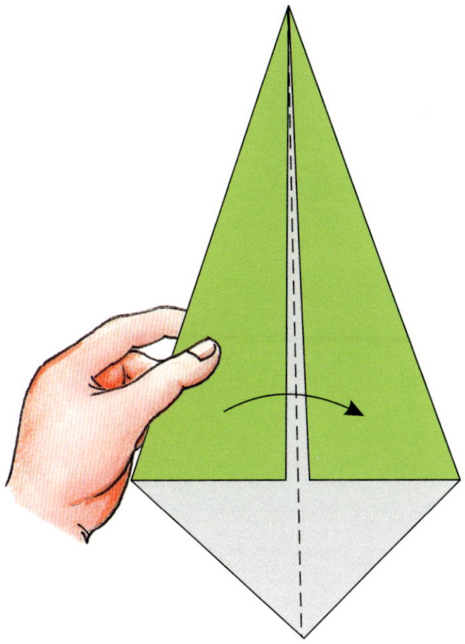

3 Now fold in half along the dotted line.

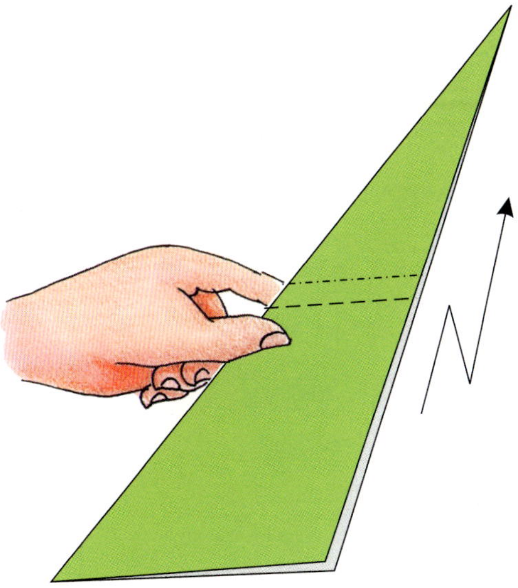

4 Make a stair-step. Fold along the dotted lines.

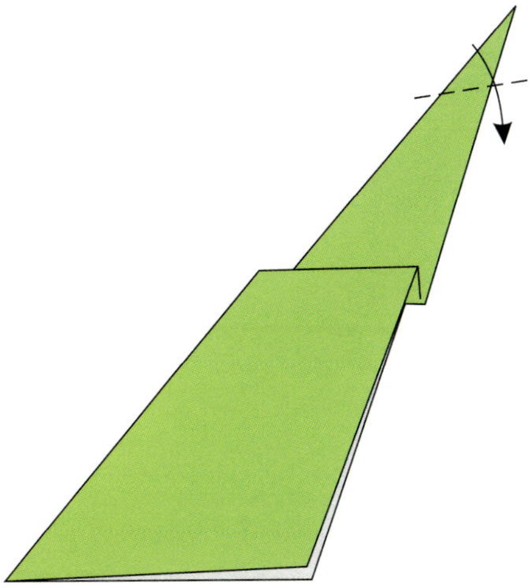

5 Now turn the top edge downward along the dotted line to make the beak of the peacock.

6 Paste a paper crown. Draw and decorate it.

Yacht

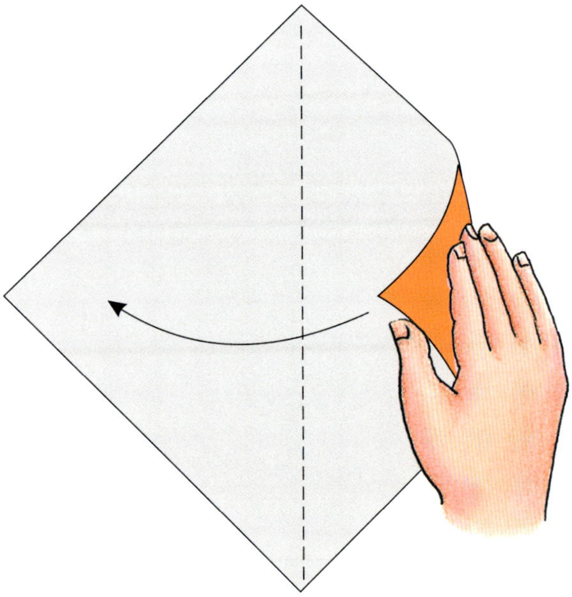

1 Fold in half along the dotted line.

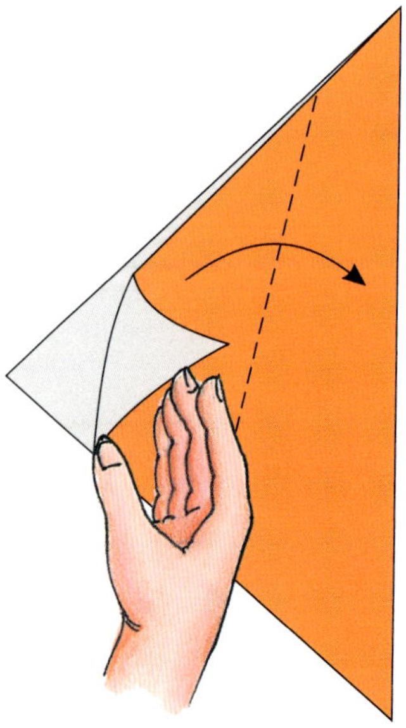

2 Fold only the upper layer upward along the dotted line.

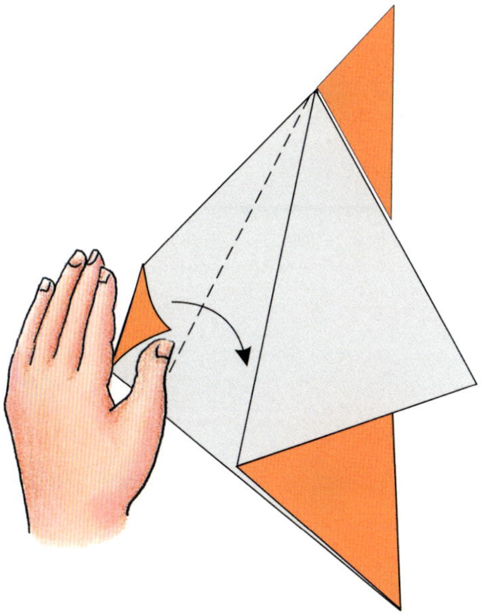

3 Now fold the lower layer upwards along the dotted line.

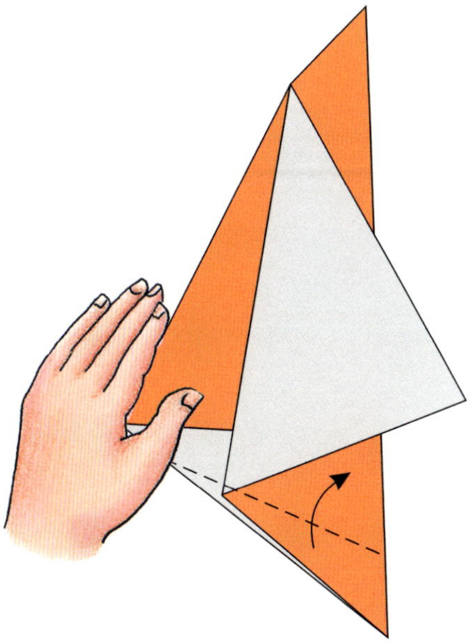

4 Fold the lower end upwards as shown.

5 Fold the bottom corner backwards as shown.

6 Your model is ready.

Pen Holder

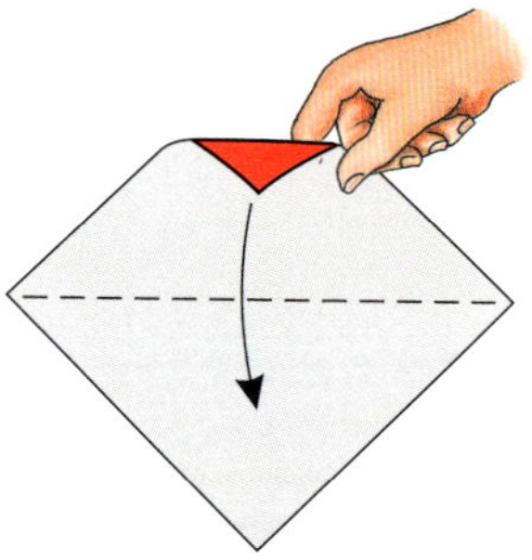

1 Make a centre crease and fold.

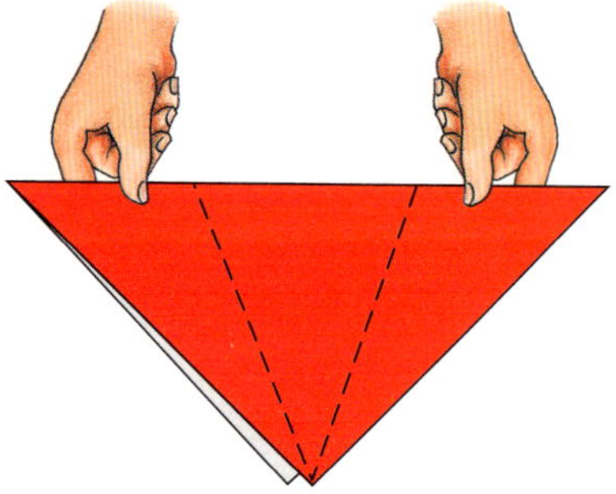

2 Draw two lines to divide the paper into three equal parts.

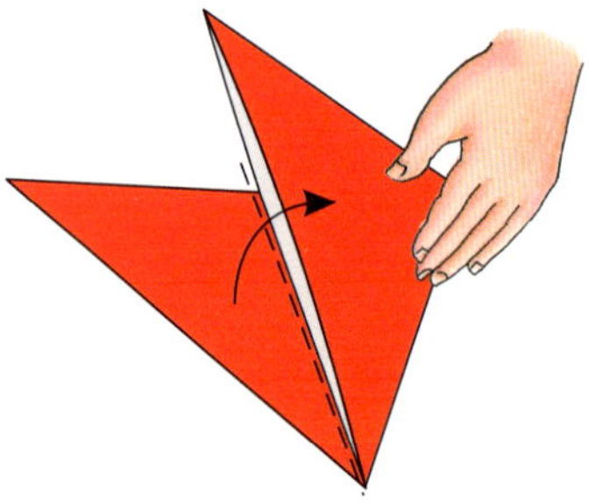

3 Fold the right flap and then the left flap along the dotted lines as shown.

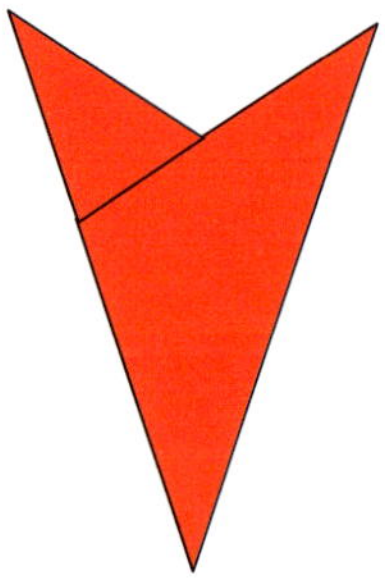

4 Your form will look like this.

5 Draw a flower to decorate it.

Hat

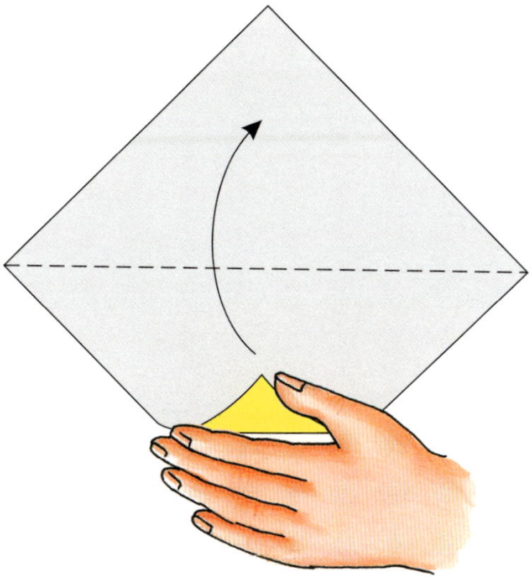

1 Make a fold along the dotted line in the direction of arrow.

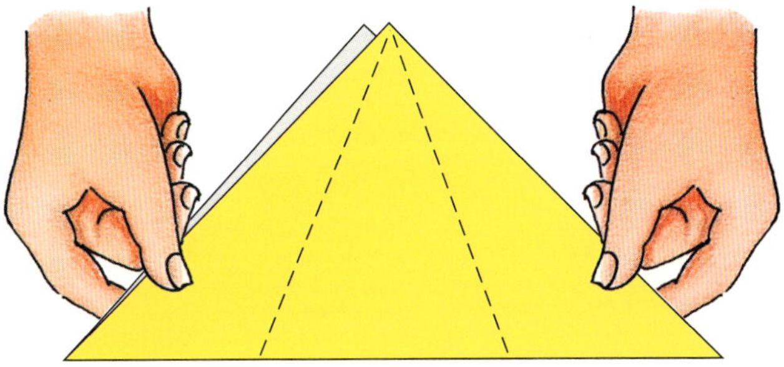

2 Draw two lines to divide the paper into three equal parts.

3 Fold the right flap and then fold the left flap along the dotted line to overlap the right flap as shown.

5 Open the hat to make it round.

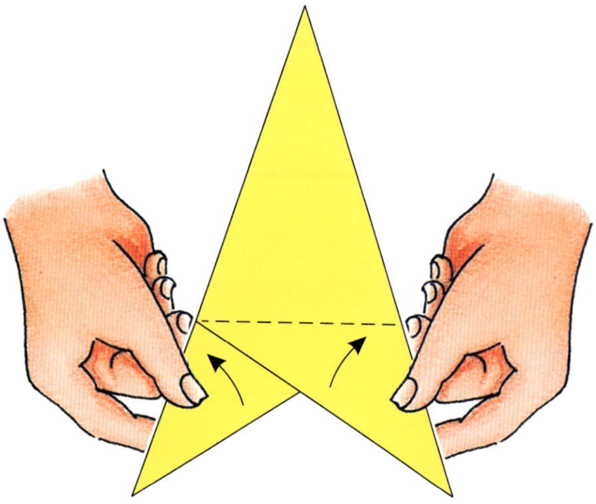

4 Fold both the corners upward along the dotted line.

6 Draw polka dots to decorate the hat.

Rabbit

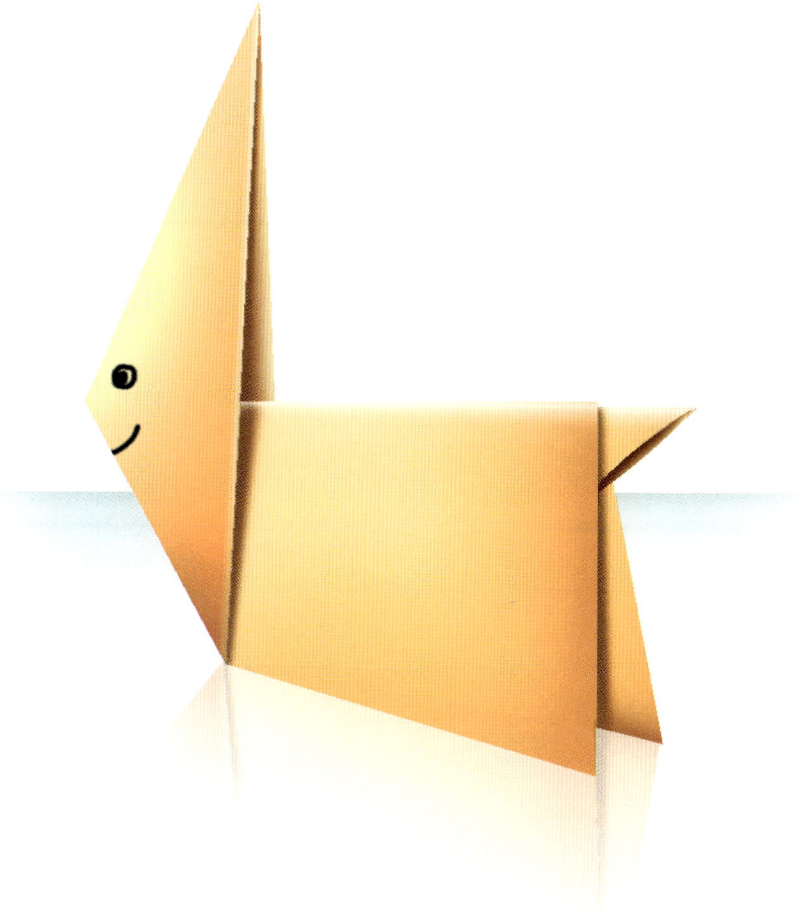

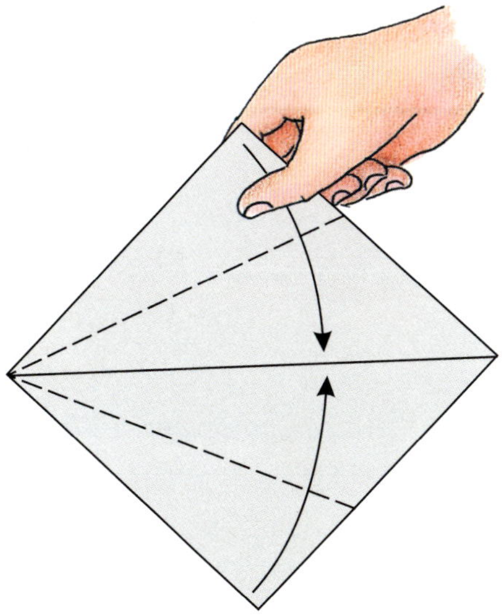

1 Make a centre crease. Now fold the top and bottom corners to the centre line.

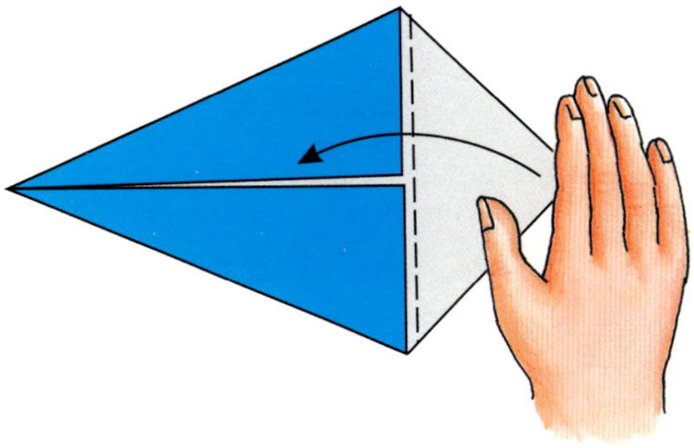

2 Fold the right corner along the dotted line as indicated.

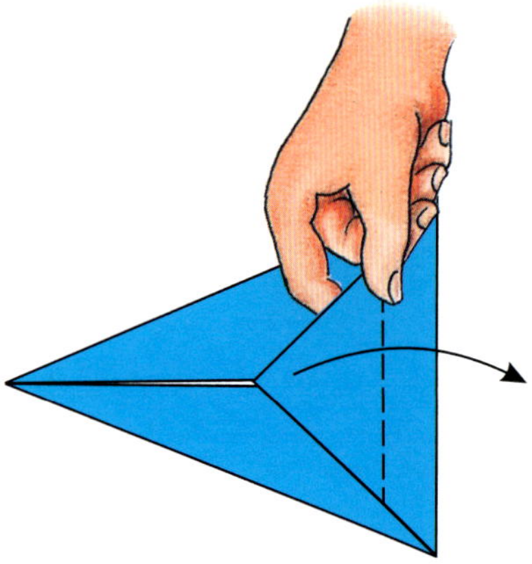

3 Now fold the flap outwards along the dotted line.

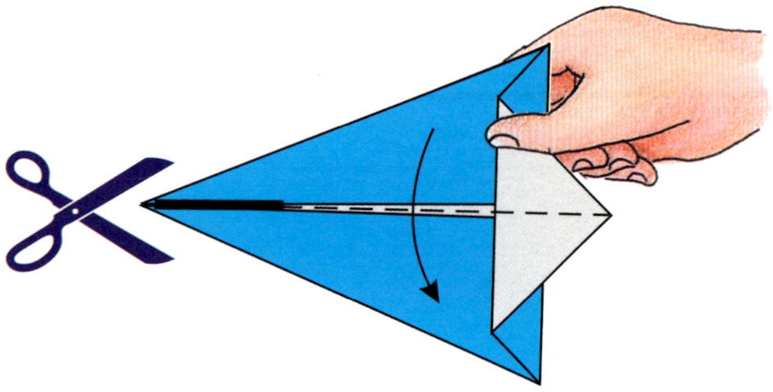

4 Make a 6 cm long cut from the left corner and fold the model in half in the direction of arrow.

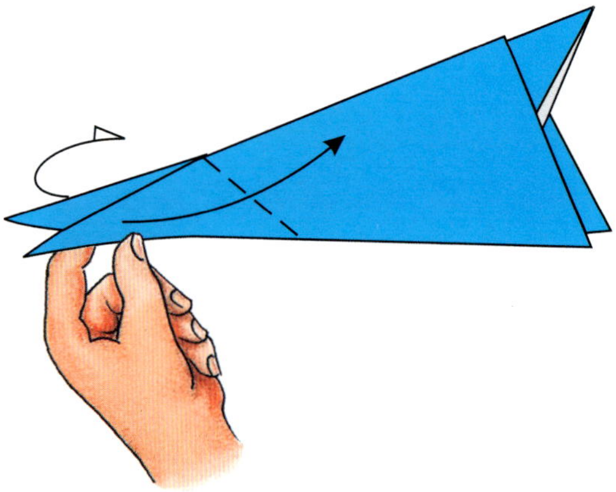

5 Fold the cut corners upwards to form the rabbit's ears as shown.

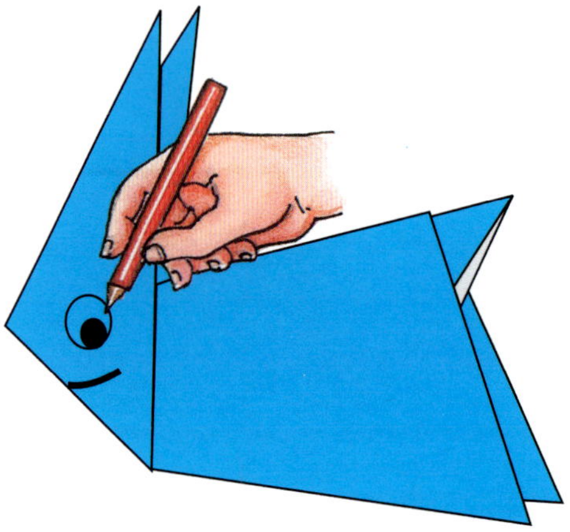

6 Draw the eyes and mouth on the face, and your rabbit is ready.

Cat cap

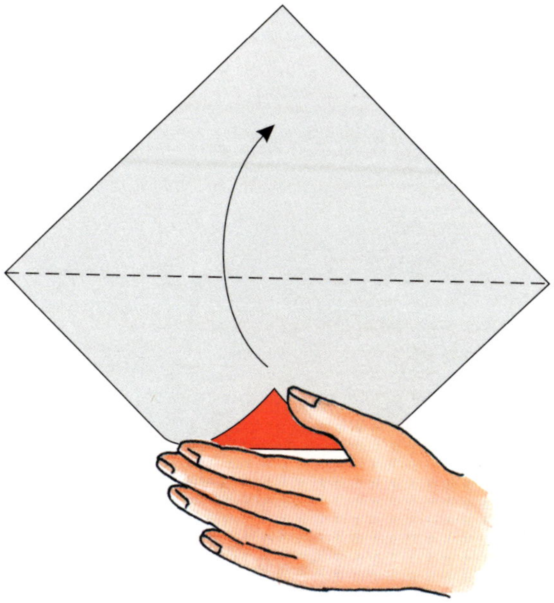

1 Make a fold along the dotted line in the direction of arrow.

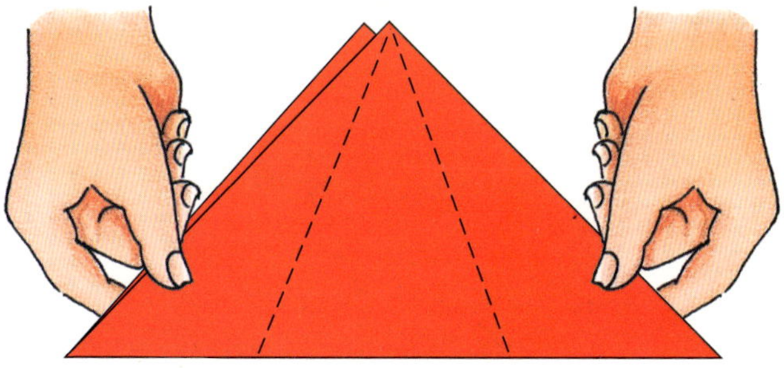

2 Draw two lines to divide the paper into three equal parts.

3 Fold the right flap and then fold the left flap along the dotted line to overlap the right flap as shown.

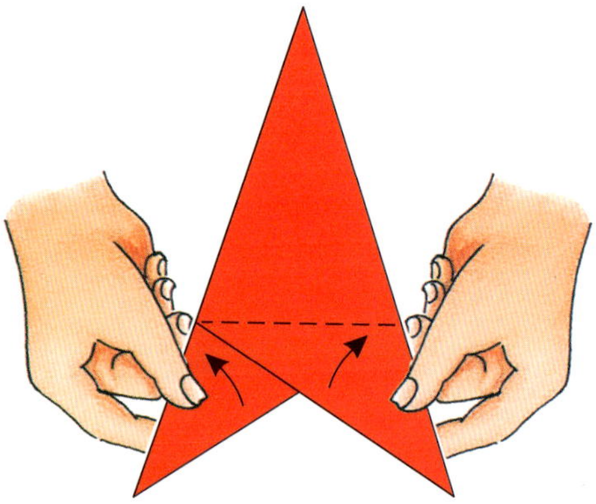

4 Fold both the corners upward along the dotted line.

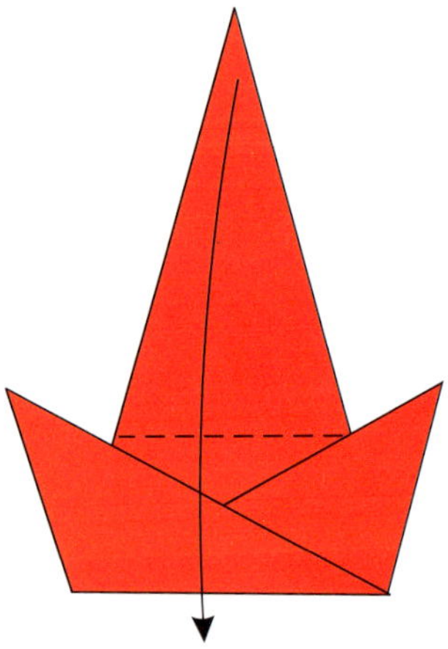

5 Fold the upper tip downwards along the dotted line.

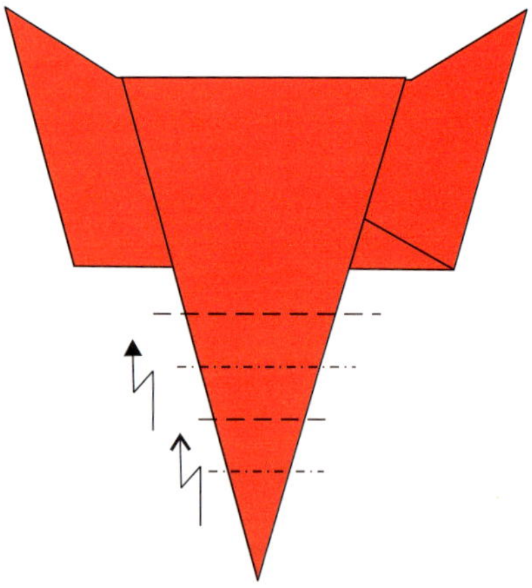

6 Fold the drooping flap forward and backward alternately.

7 Draw eyes and whiskers like this. The cat cap is ready.

Collage Work

TIPS AND TRICKS

Step-1 Collect paper sheets of various colours of your own choice. Tear them in small pieces of different shapes.

Step-2 Set them within the outline and paste in the given shape.

Yacht

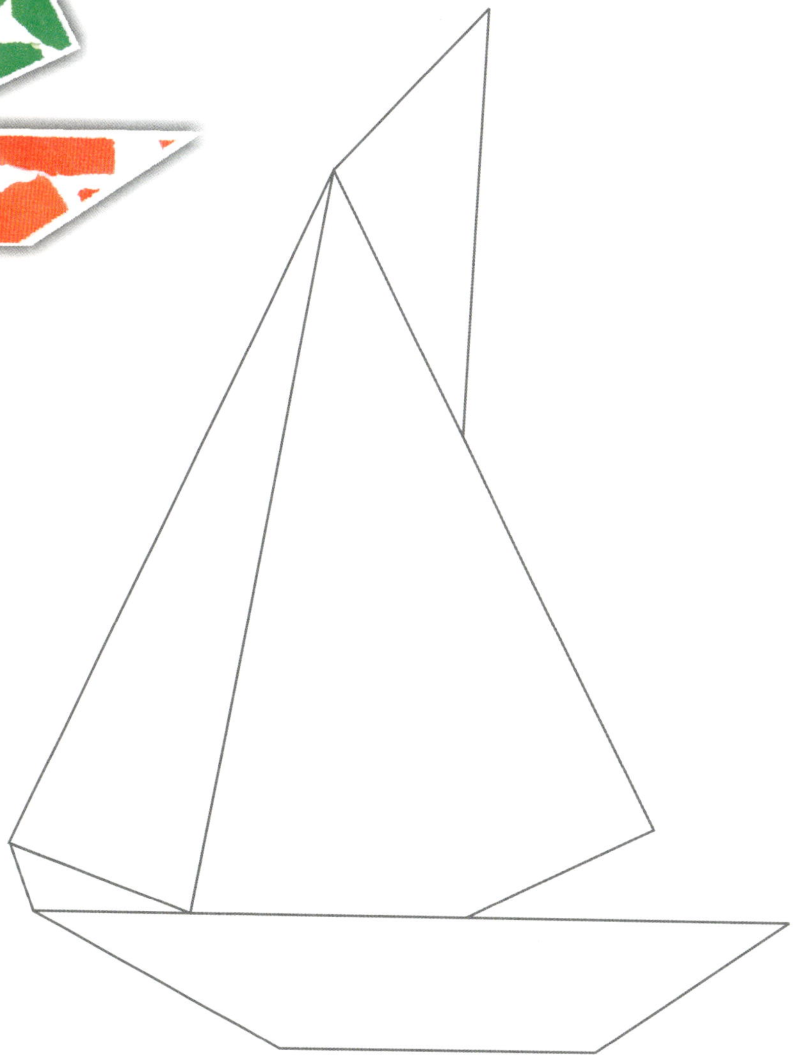

Cut and Paste

Cat Cap

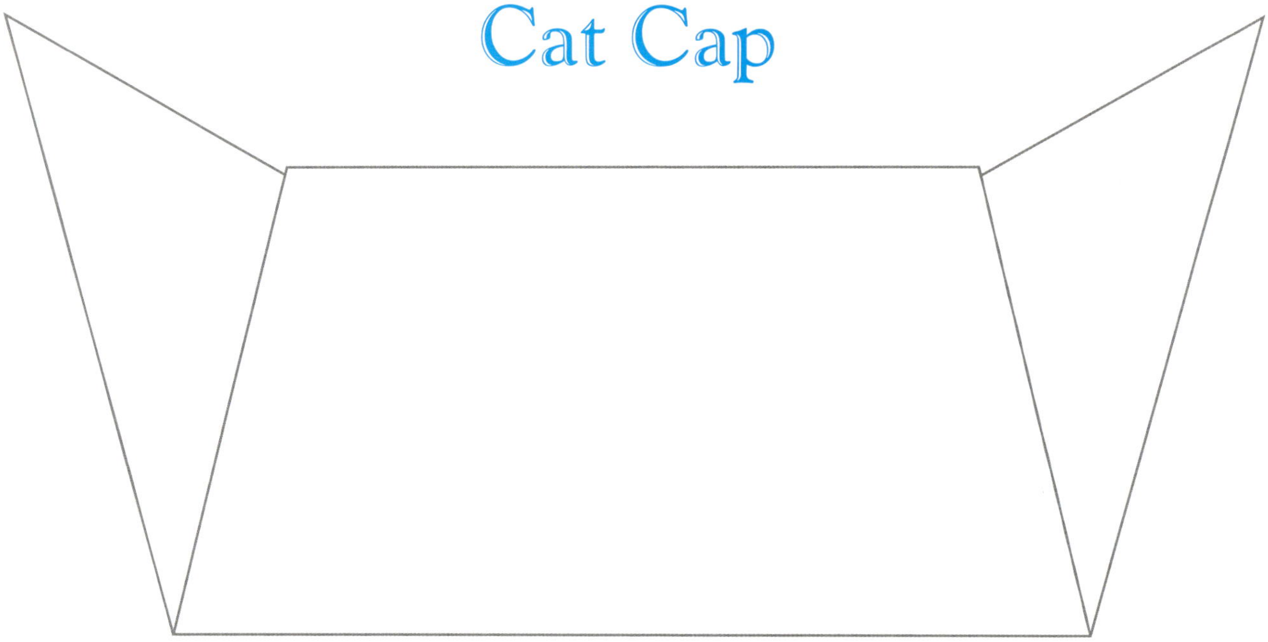

TIPS AND TRICKS

Step-1 Take craft paper sheets of various colours. Trace different parts on the shape of different colours.

Step-2 Now paste these pieces at the appropriate places.

Crushed Paper Art

TIPS AND TRICKS

Step-1 Take a plain paper and squeeze it in your hand. Open it gently and apply the poster colour with a flat brush.

Step-2 Now cut the paper according to the shape and paste it within the outline.

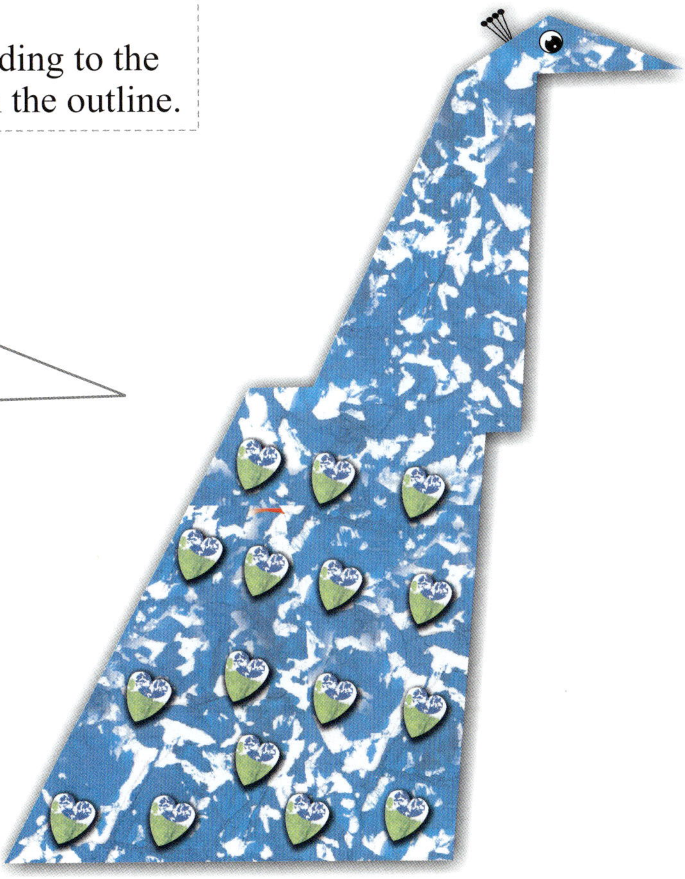

Peacock

Spray Paint

TIPS AND TRICKS

Step-1 Take a white paper. Spray different colours of your own choice with a tooth brush on the white paper.

Step-2 Cut the parts of the shape as per your liking and paste them on the figure.

Hat

Air Wheel

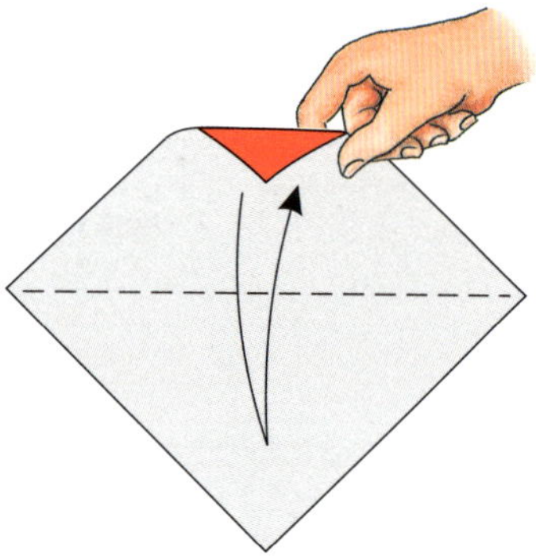

1 Make a centre crease and unfold.

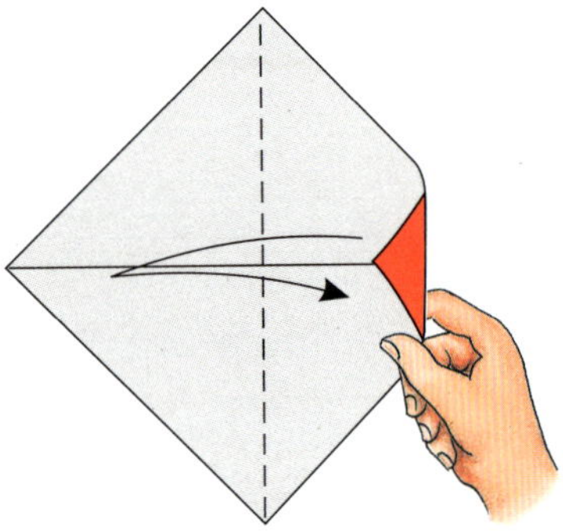

2 Make another crease and unfold.

3 Cut the four corners as shown.

4 Fold and paste the alternate corners at the mid-point.

5 Fix the air wheel to a stick with the help of a pin and see how it rolls.

Sweet Box

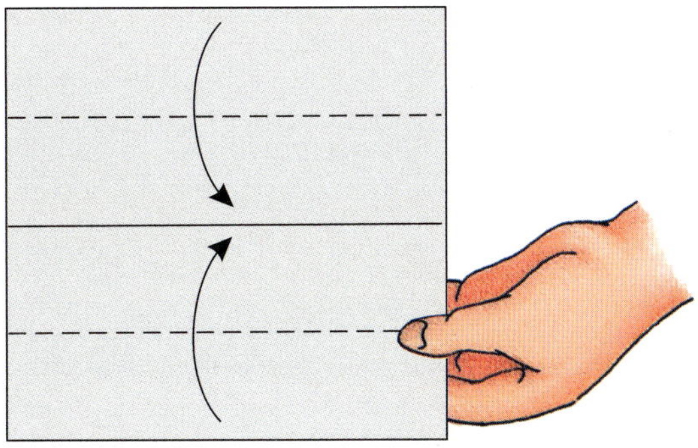

1 Fold the upper and lower edges to the centre line.

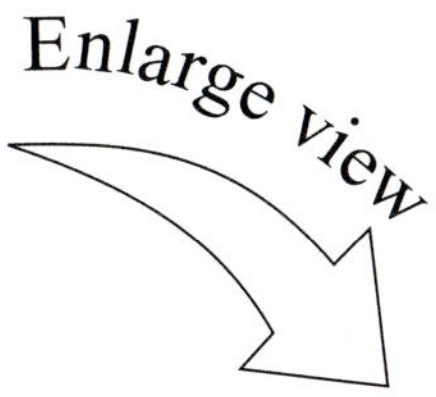

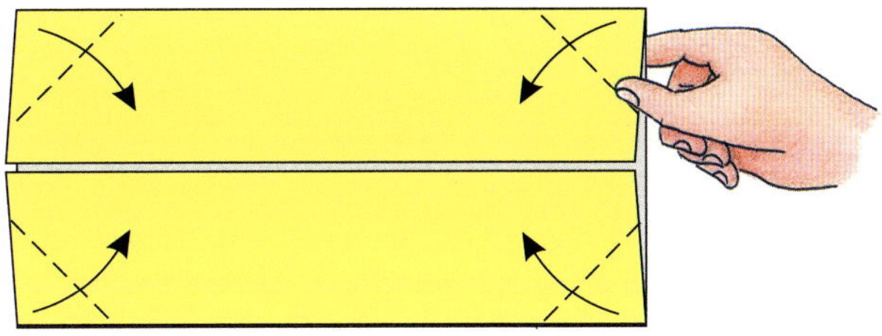

2 Now, fold all the four corners inward along the dotted lines.

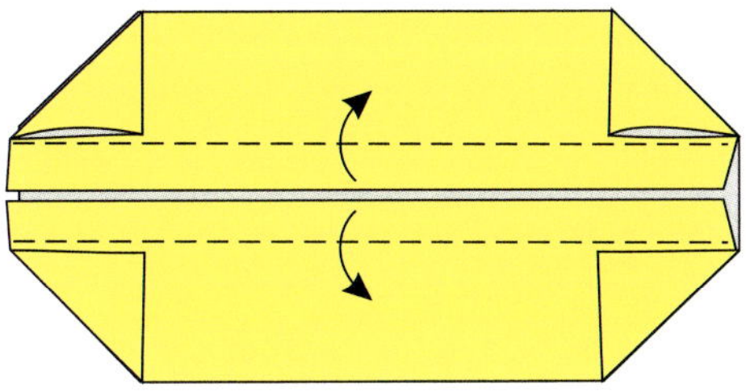

3 Fold the flaps from the centre line to overlap the triangles.

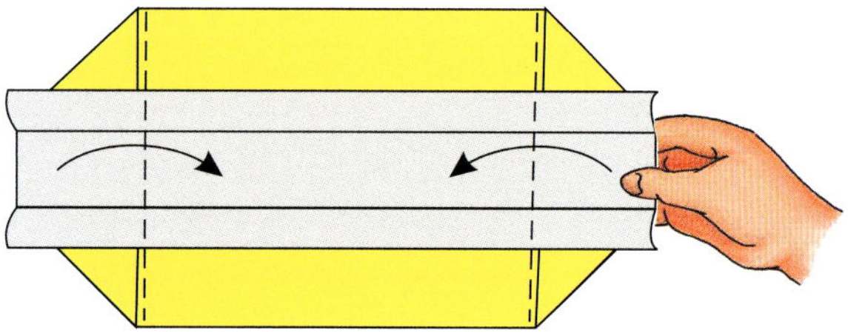

4 Fold the left and right flaps along the dotted lines and make them stand vertically.

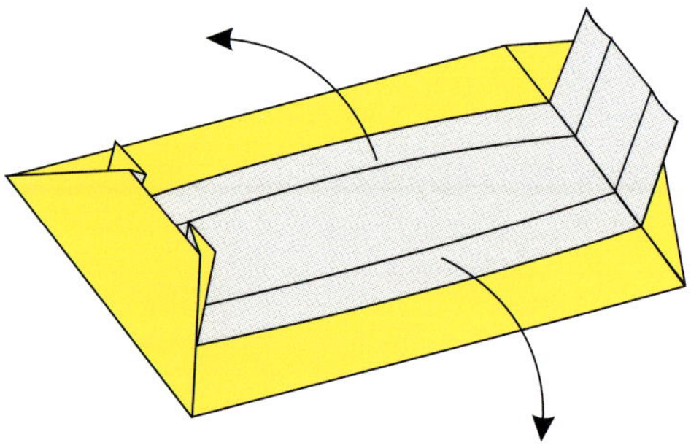

5 Open both the sides outwards in the direction of arrows.

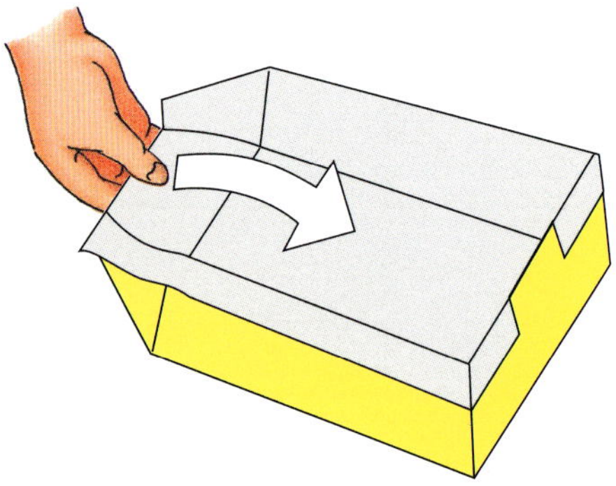

6 Now, push left and right sides inside to shape the box....

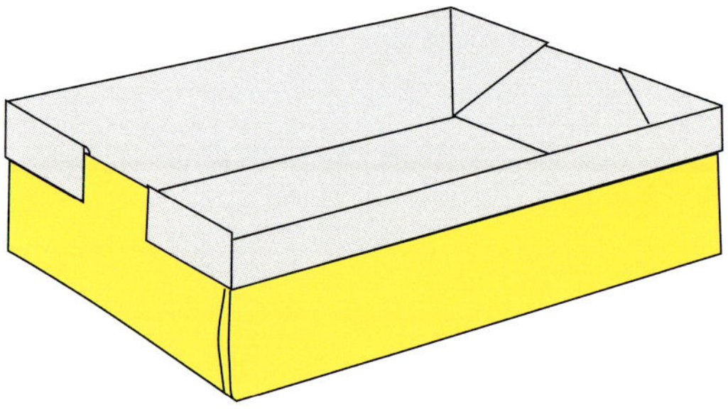

7 .... like this, and your sweet box is ready.

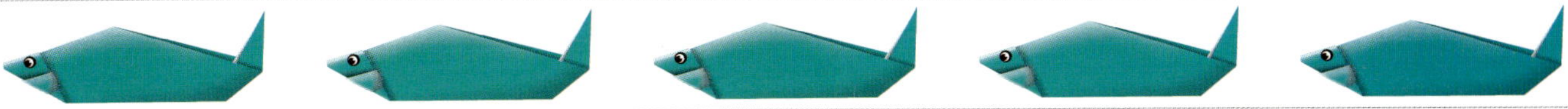

Sea Fish

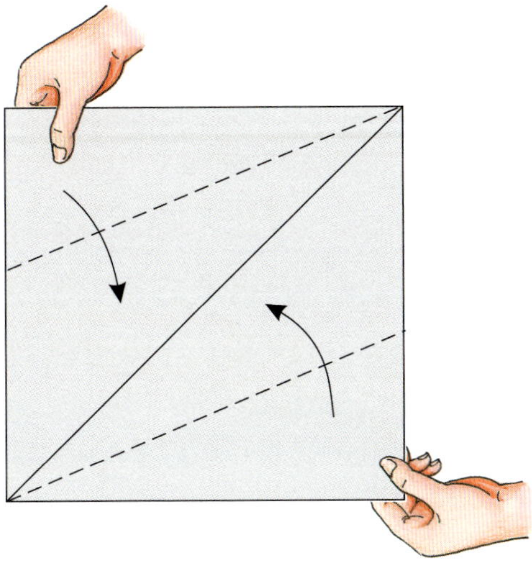

1 Make folds up to the centre line along the dotted lines in the direction of arrows.

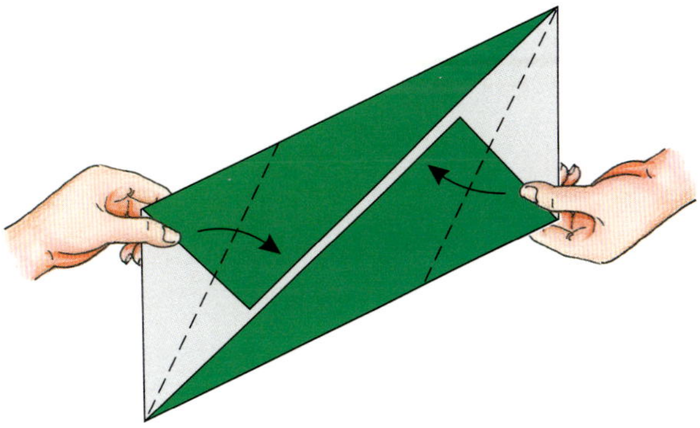

2 Fold both the corners inside along the dotted lines.

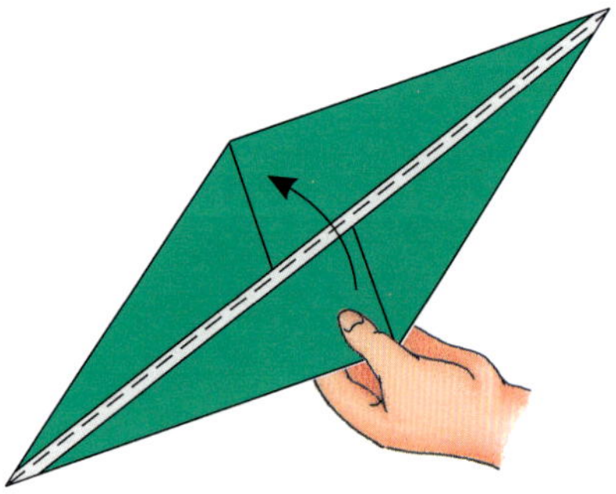

3 Fold in half upward along the dotted line.

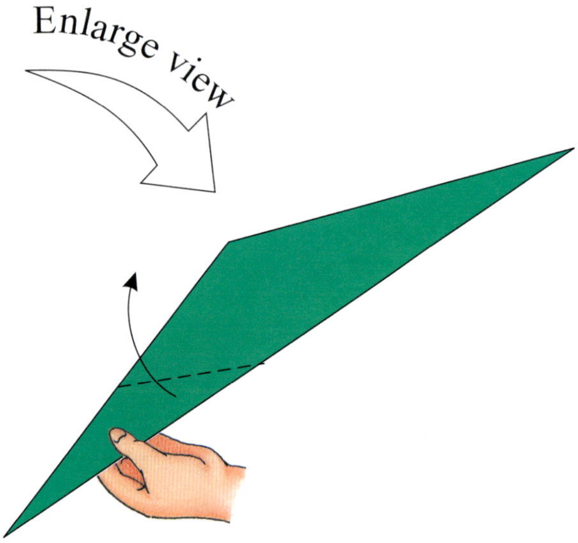

4 Fold upward along the dotted line.

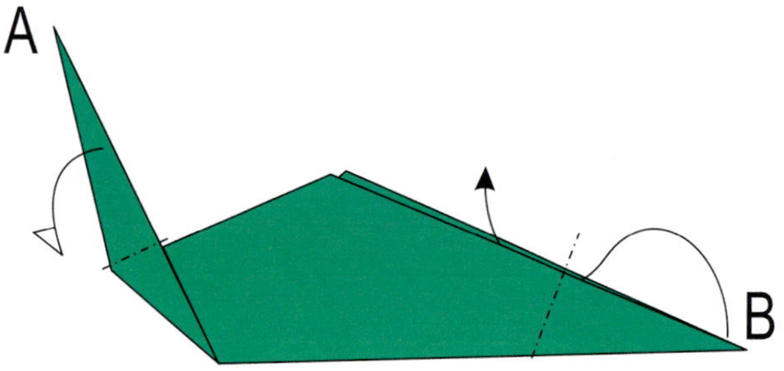

5 Fold the point 'A' backward in the direction of arrow. Make a pocket fold at point 'B'....

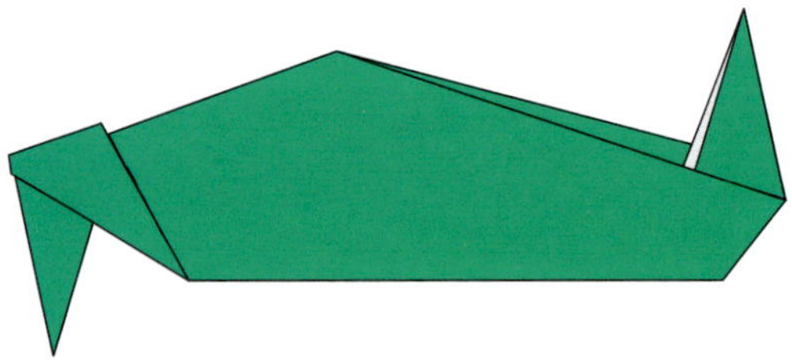

6 Push the left corner inside the form as shown.

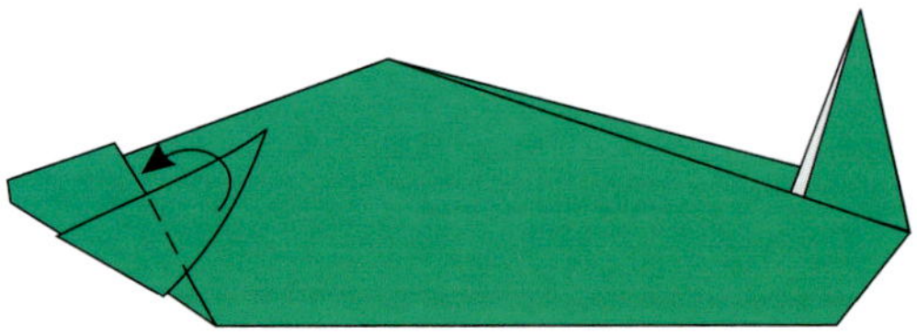

7 ....like this.

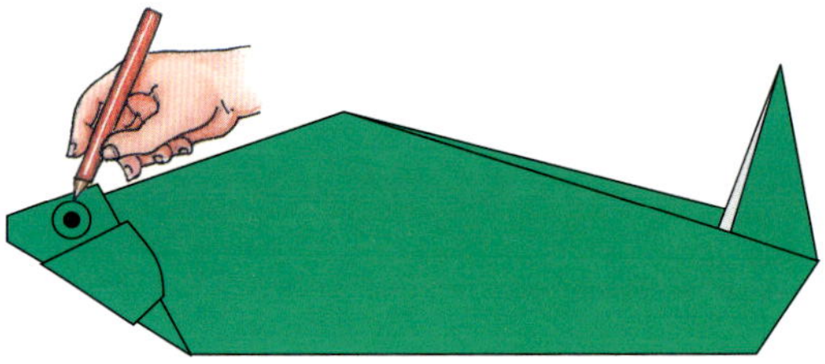

8 Draw an eye. Now, your fish is ready to go into the water.

Penguin

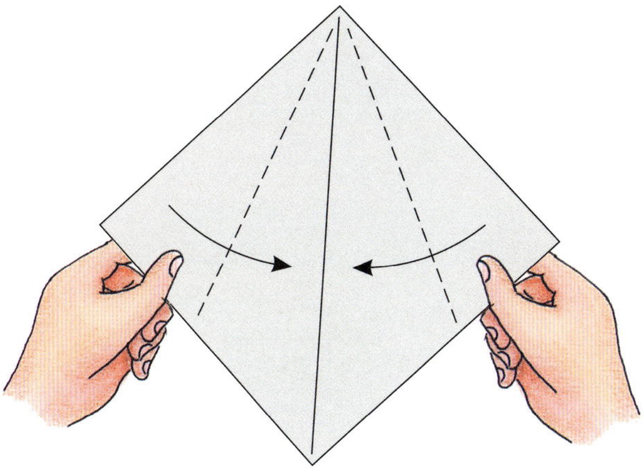

1 Fold the right and left corners to the centre line.

2 Fold in half backwards.

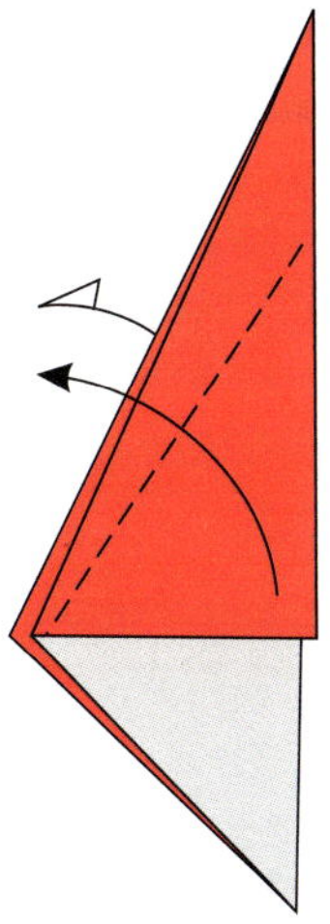

3 Fold both the triangular flaps outwards....

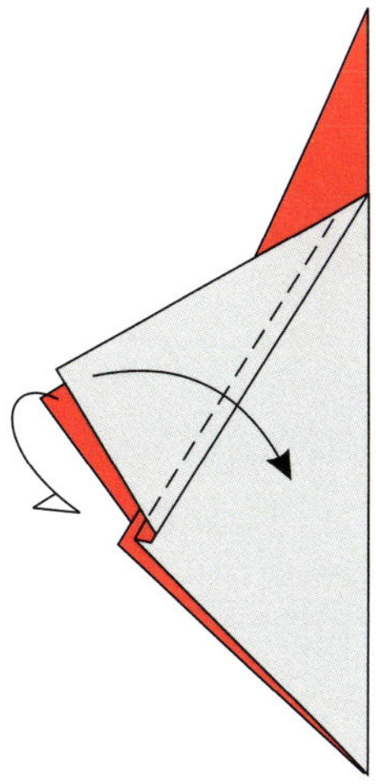

4 .... and inwards along the dotted line.

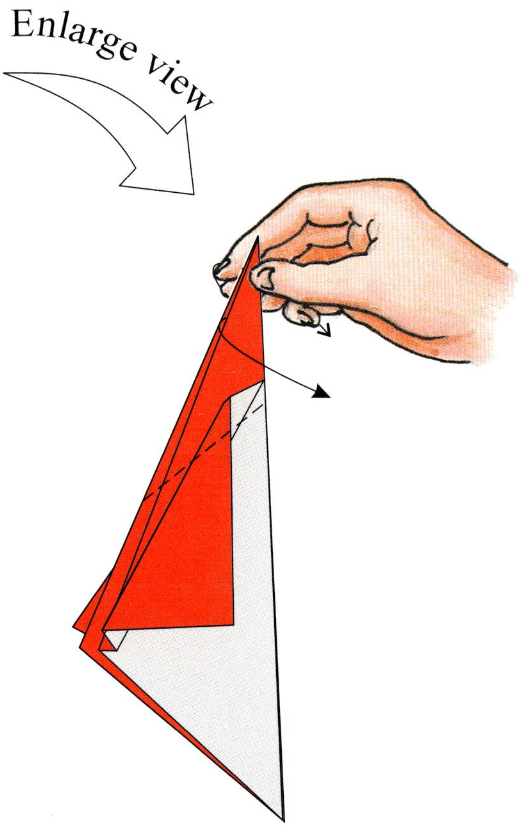

5 Make a hood fold at the upper tip for the head.

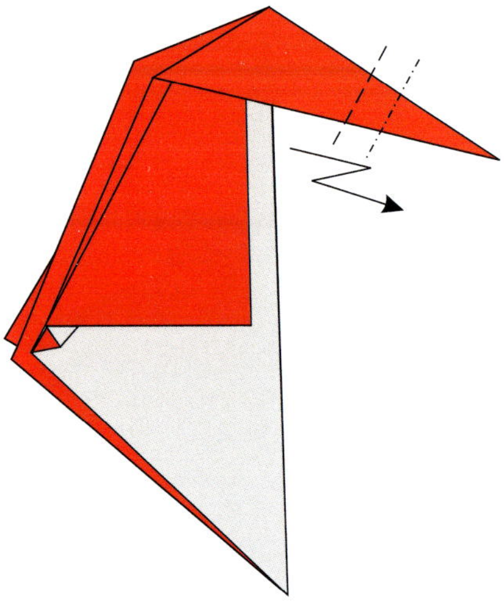

6 Make a stair-step fold for the beak.

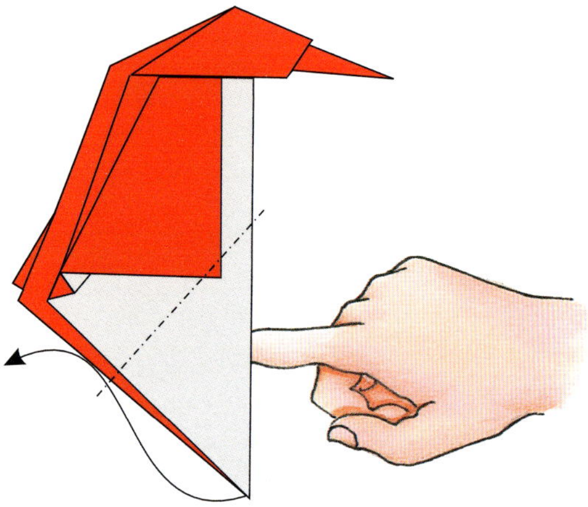

7 Make a pocket fold at the lower tip.

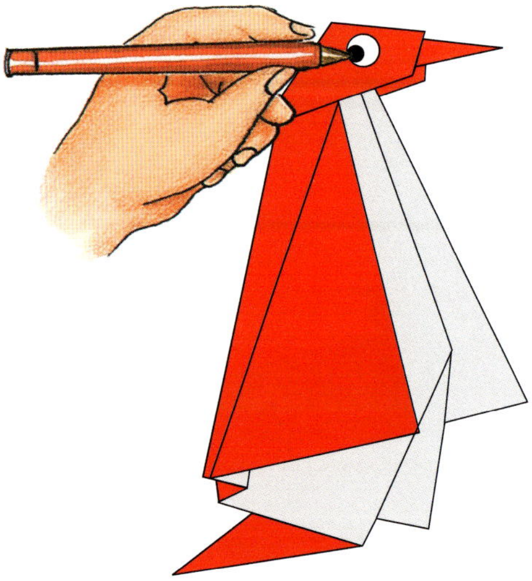

8 Draw eyes on the face and your penguin is ready.

Swan

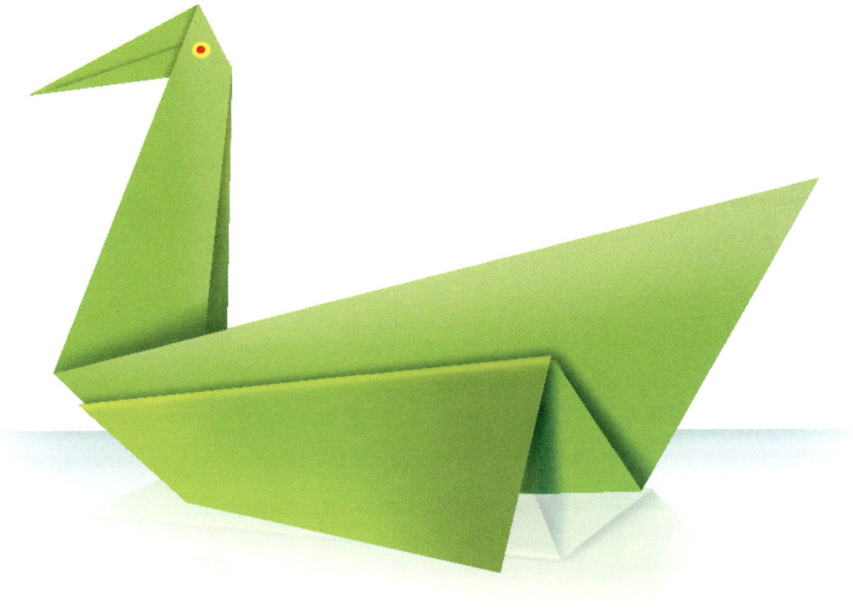

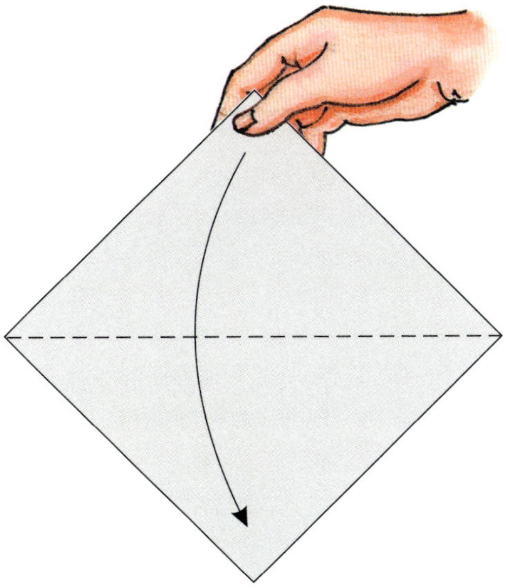

1 Fold in half along the dotted line.

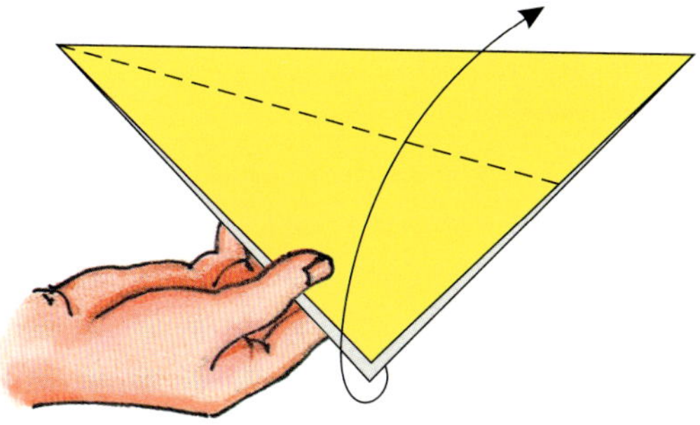

2 Fold both the layers upward along the dotted line.

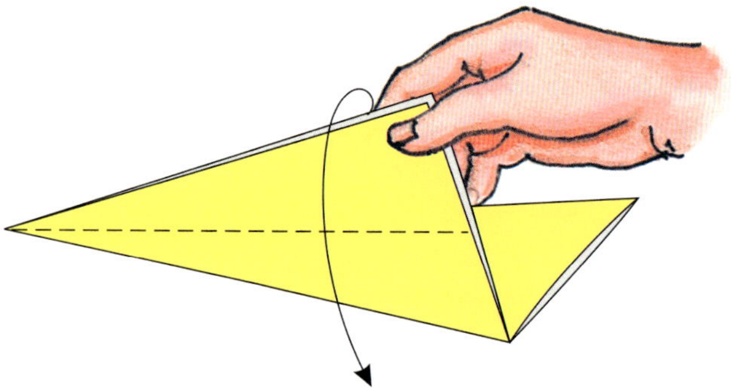

3 Now, fold both the layers downward along the dotted line.

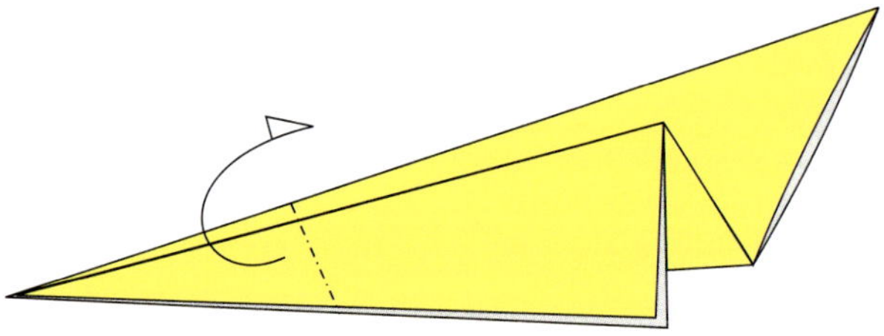

4 Fold the tip backwards to form the swan's neck.

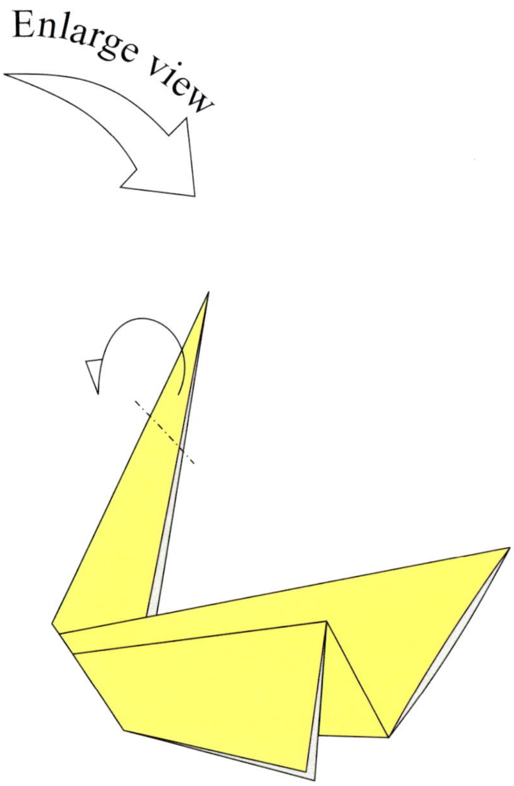

5 Fold the top corner backwards to form its head.

6 Draw an eye and your swan is ready.

Mouse

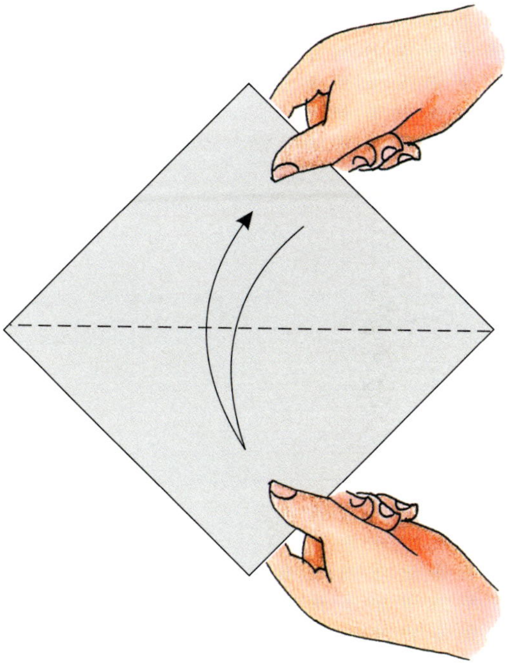

1 Make a centre crease and unfold.

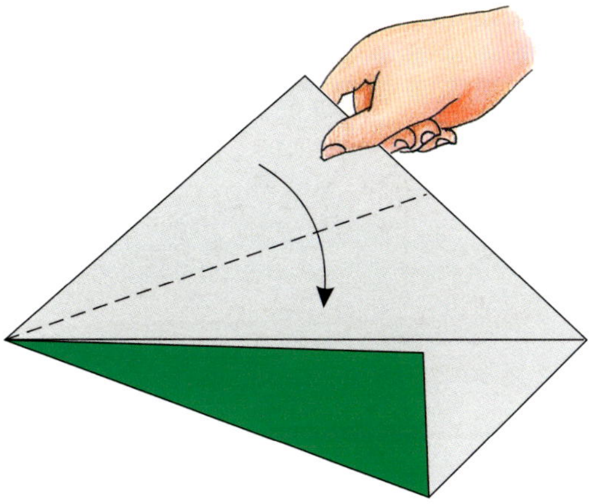

2 Fold the top and bottom corners upto the centre crease.

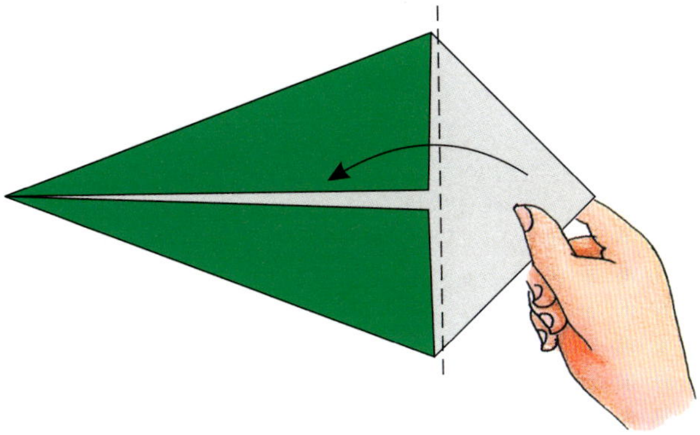

3 Fold the right corner inward along the dotted line.

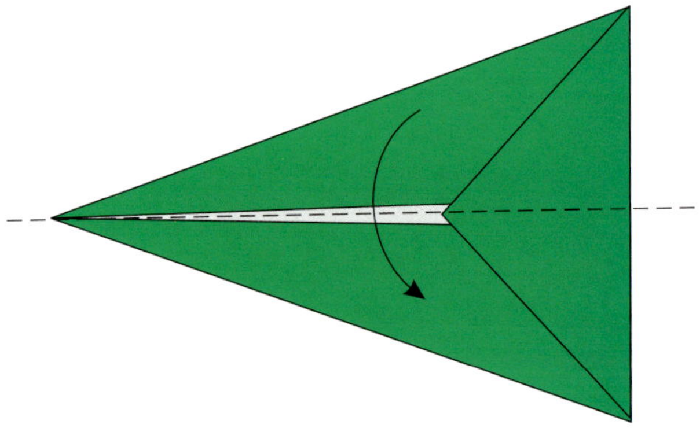

4 Now fold in half along the dotted line....

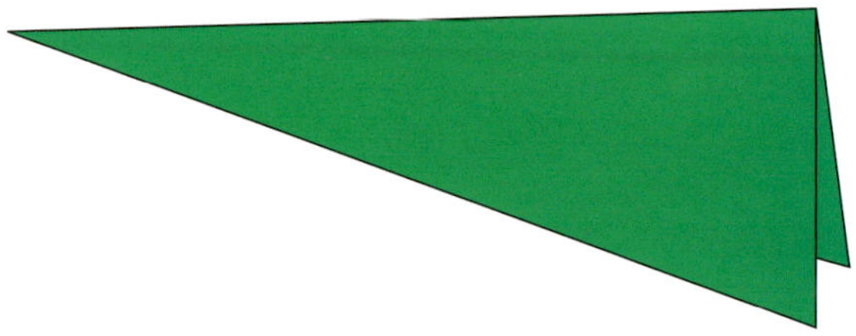

5 ....to make the form of this type.

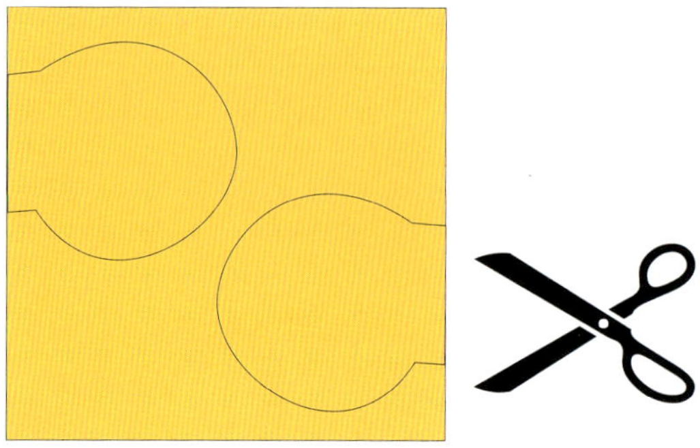

6 Cut two small round pieces of a different coloured paper for ears....

7 .... and paste them as shown. Draw eyes and whiskers. Finally, paste a piece of ribbon for the tail.

Pencil Holder

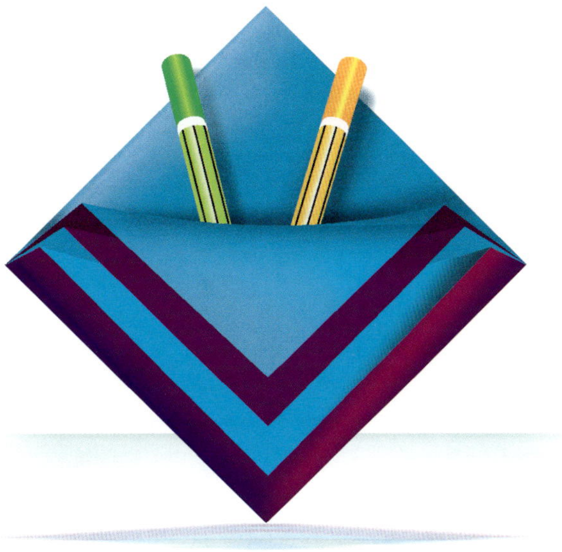

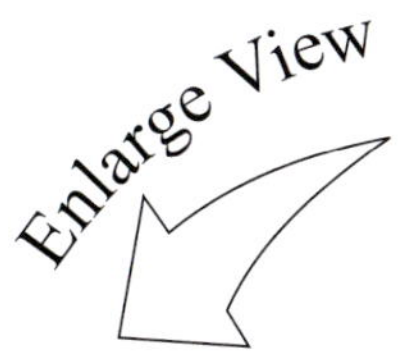

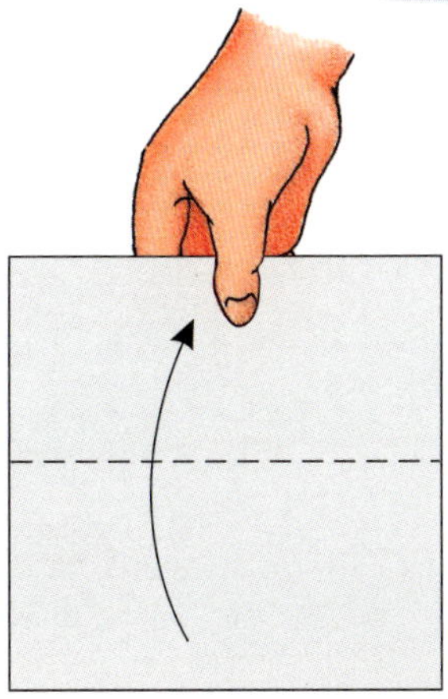

1 Fold in half along the dotted line as shown.

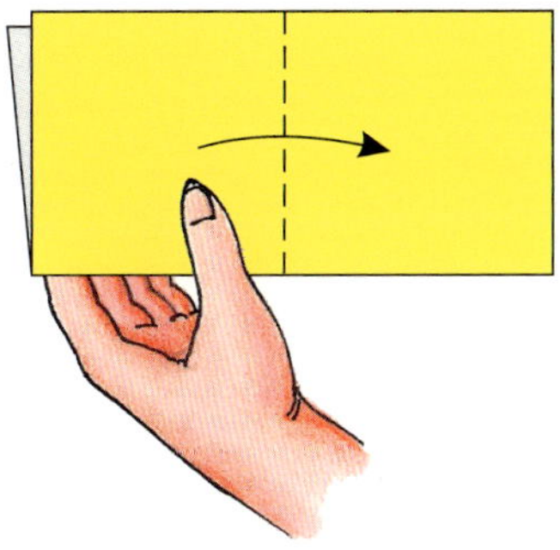

2 Again fold in half along the dotted line.

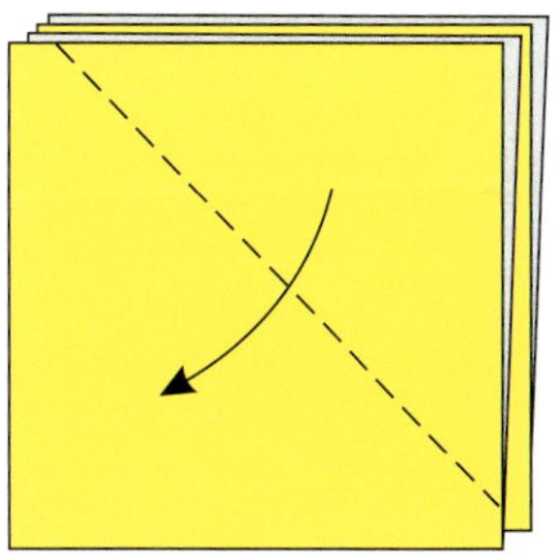

3 Fold the upper flap along the dotted line as shown.

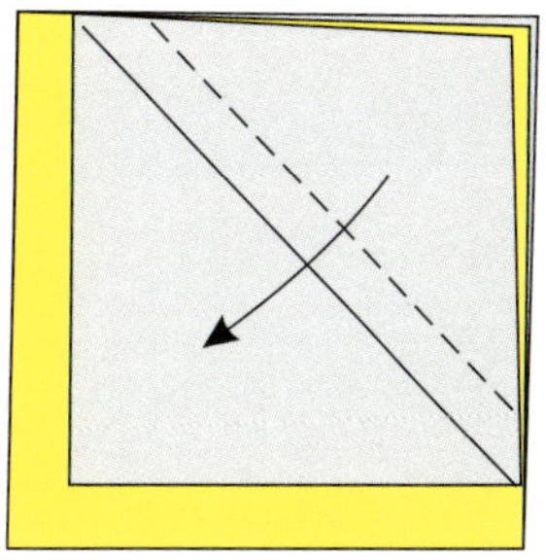

4 Fold the second flap along the dotted line.

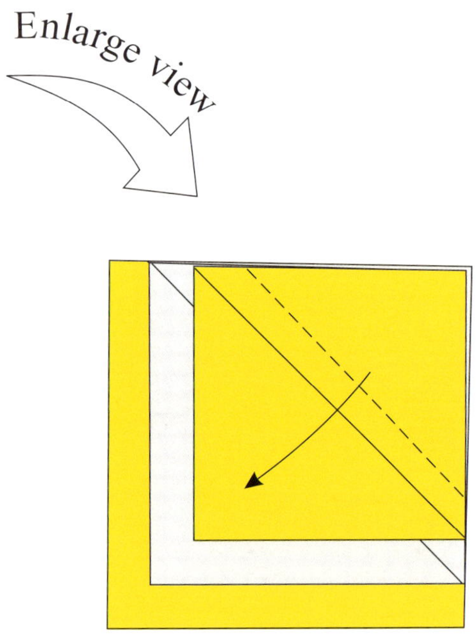

5 Similarly, fold the third flap....

6 … like this.

7 Insert your fingers in the pocket to give it a proper shape and tilt it slightly.

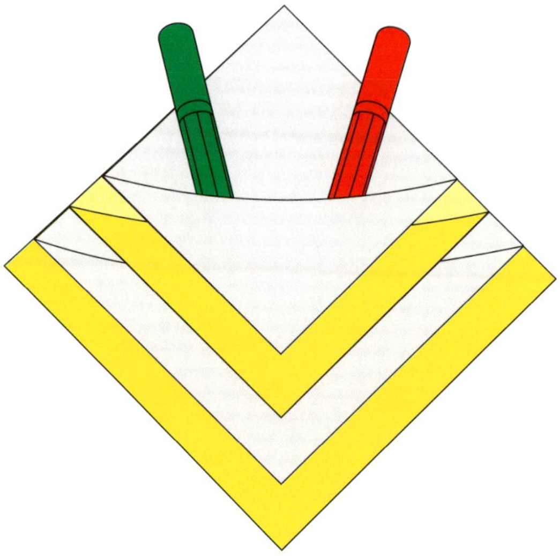

8 Your pencil box is ready. You can put your pencils in it.

Collage Work

Swan

TIPS AND TRICKS

Step-1 Collect paper sheets of various colours of your own choice. Tear them in small pieces of different shapes.

Step-2 Set them within the outline and paste in the given shape.

Cut and Paste

Sea-Fish

TIPS AND TRICKS

Step-1 Take craft paper sheets of various colours. Trace different parts on the shape of different colours.

Step-2 Now paste these pieces at the appropriate places.

Crushed Paper Art

Penguin

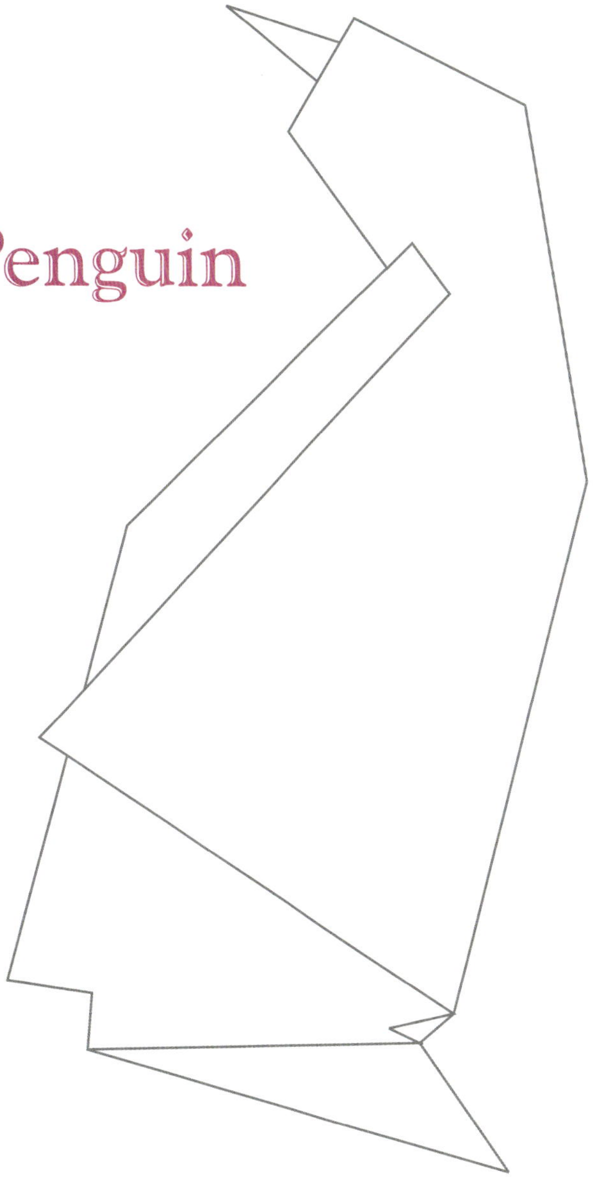

TIPS AND TRICKS

Step-1 Take a plain paper and squeeze it in your hand. Open it gently and apply the poster colour with a flat brush.

Step-2 Now cut the paper according to the shape and paste it within the outline.

Spray Paint

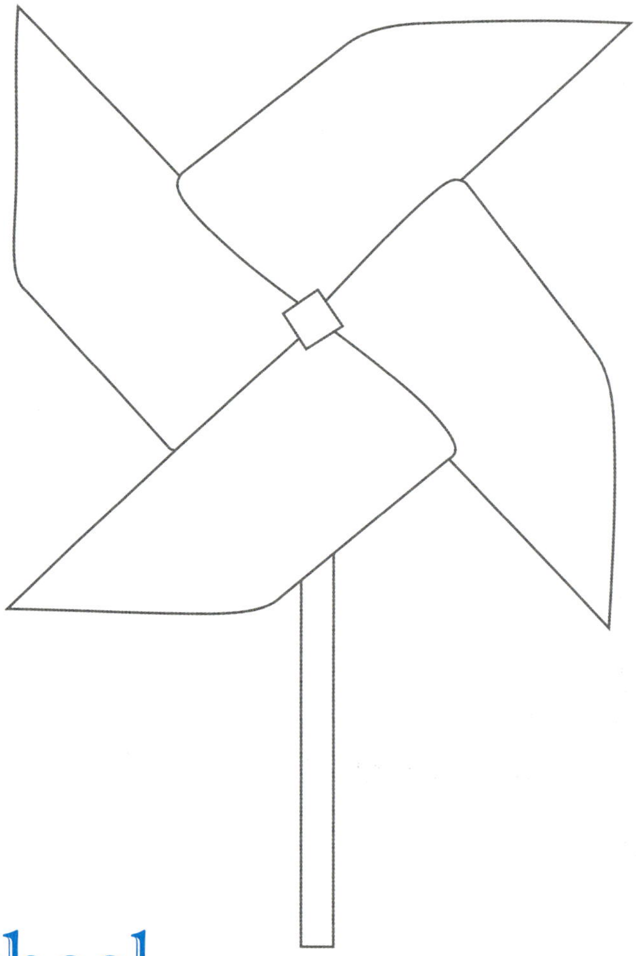

Air wheel

TIPS AND TRICKS

Step-1 Take a white paper. Spray different colours of your own choice with a tooth brush on the white paper.

Step-2 Cut the parts of the shape as per your liking and paste them on the figure.

Fox Head

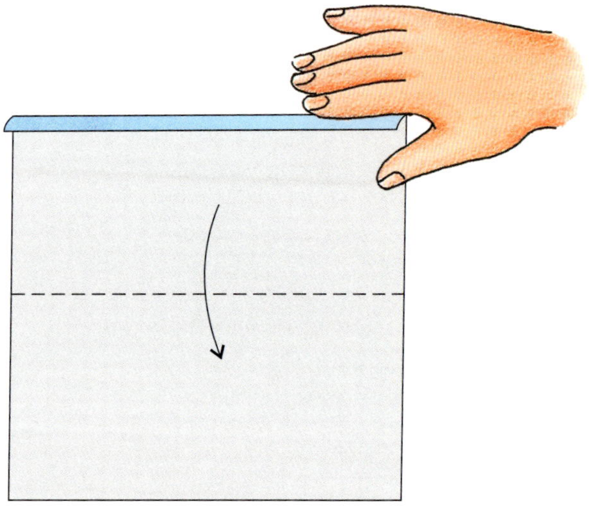

1 Fold in half along the dotted line.

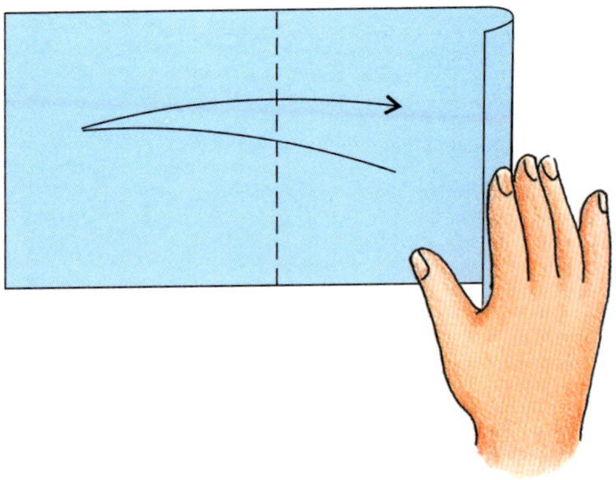

2 Fold in half and unfold to get the centre crease.

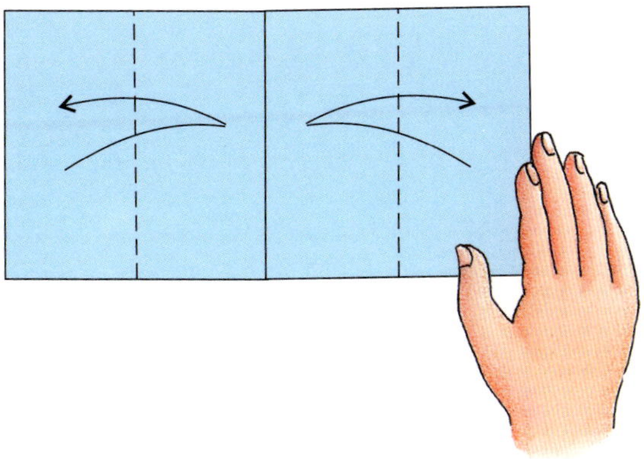

3 Fold the right and the left sides to the centre line and unfold.

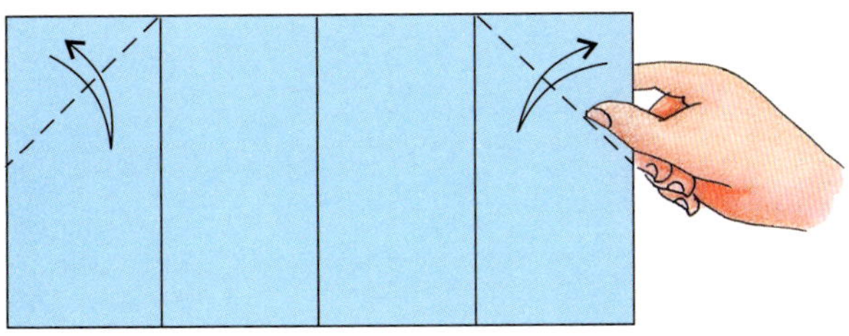

4 Fold the top corners forward and backward and unfold.

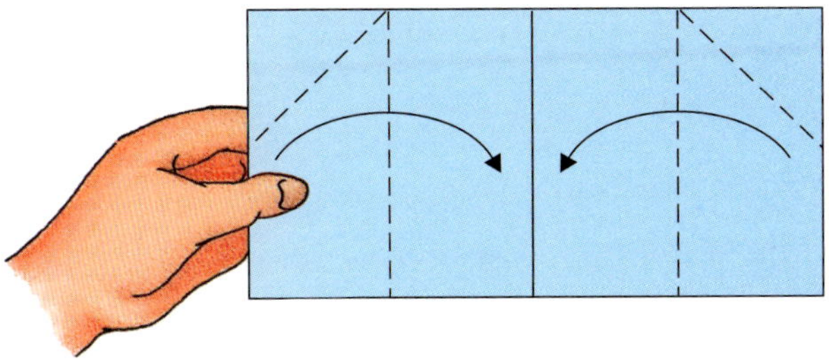

5 Fold both the sides along the dotted lines.

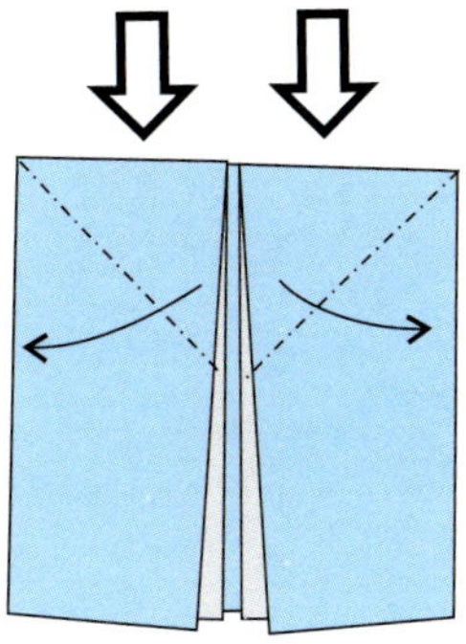

6 Open the upper layers to the left and right as shown and press the upper edges.

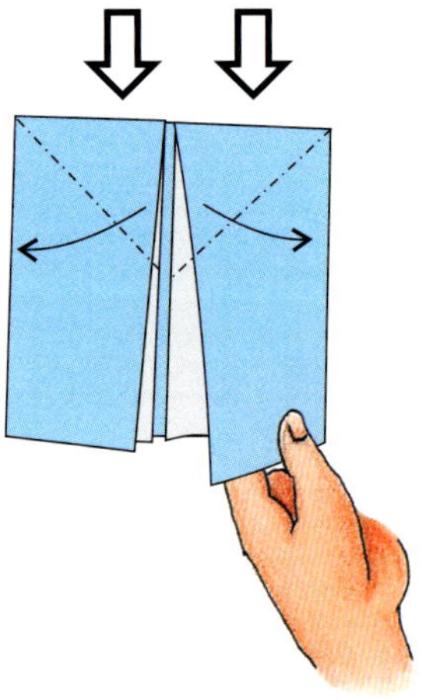

7 It opens out into triangles when flattened.

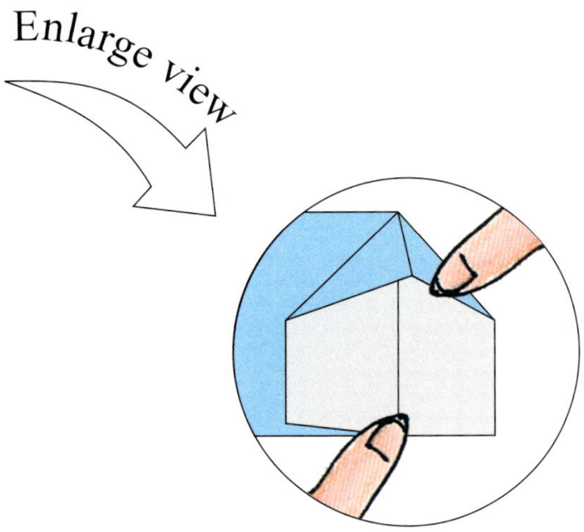

8 … like this.

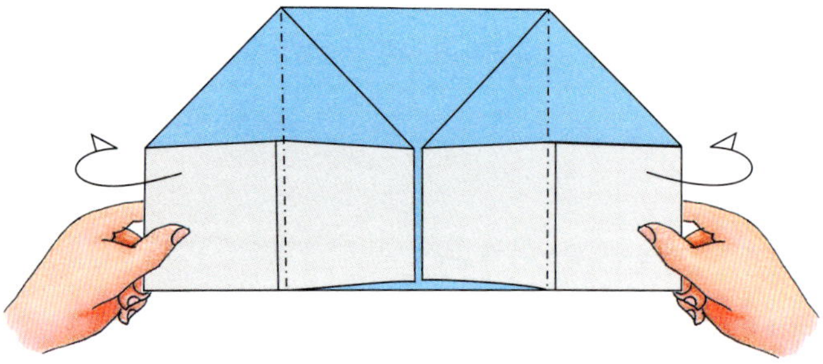

9 Fold the side flaps backwards.

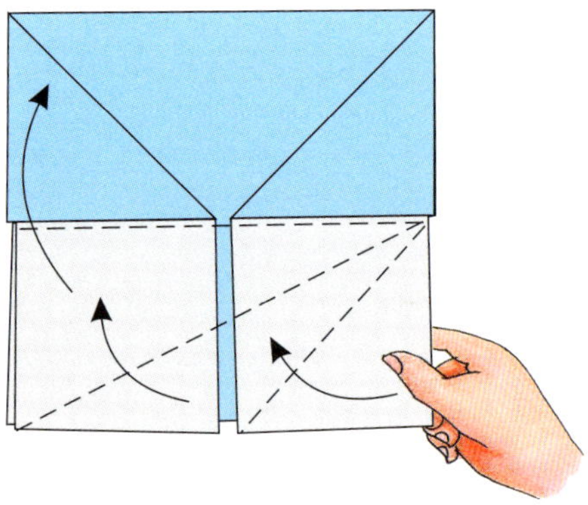

10 Make three folds of the upper layer....

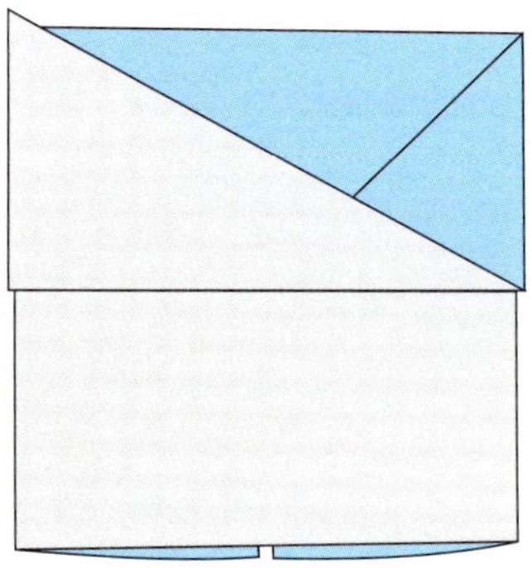

11 ..... like this.

12 Again make three folds of this layer....

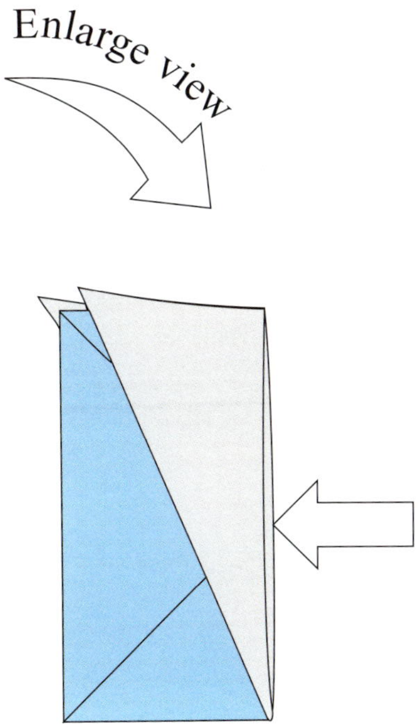

13 ..... like this.

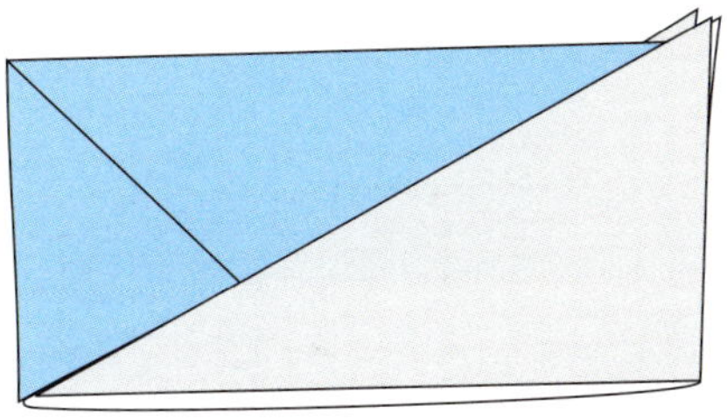

14 Hold the model vertically and insert your fingers in the pocket.

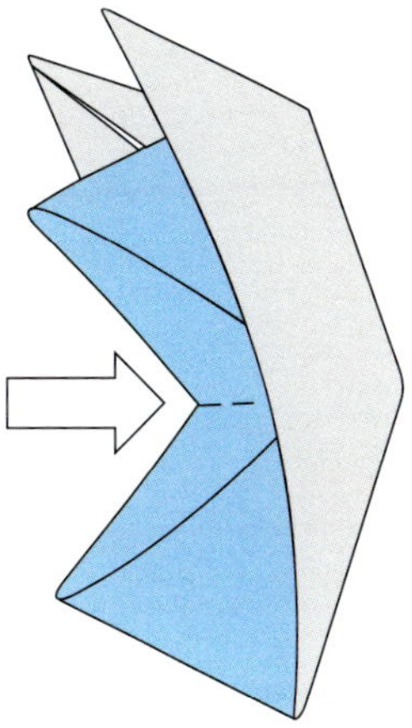

15 Push the middle portion inside to form mouth and crease the line firmly. Now draw eyes and nose on it.

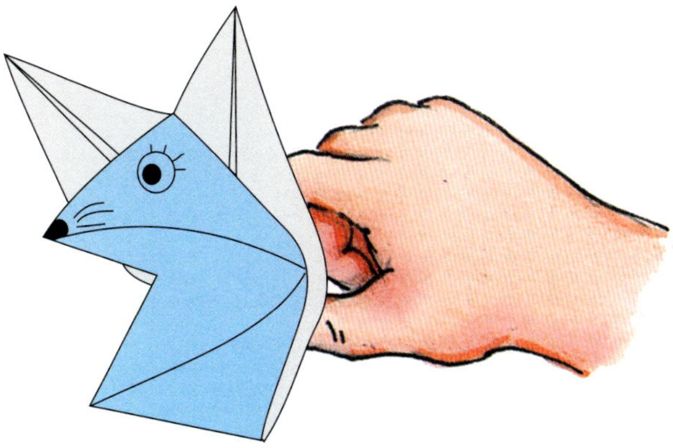

16 Insert the fingers and the thumb to open and close the mouth.

Softy

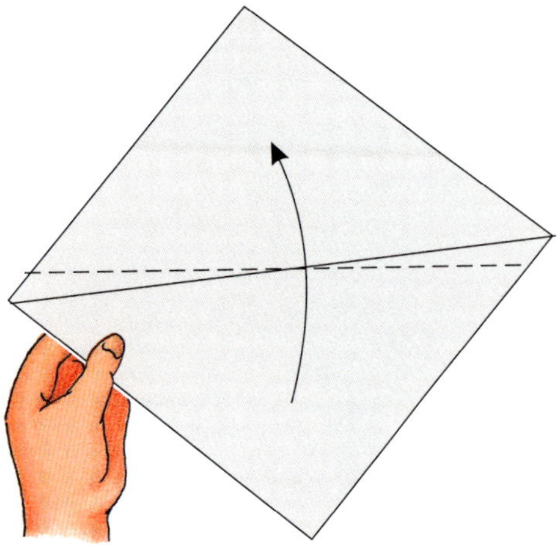

1 Fold carefully along the dotted line as shown.

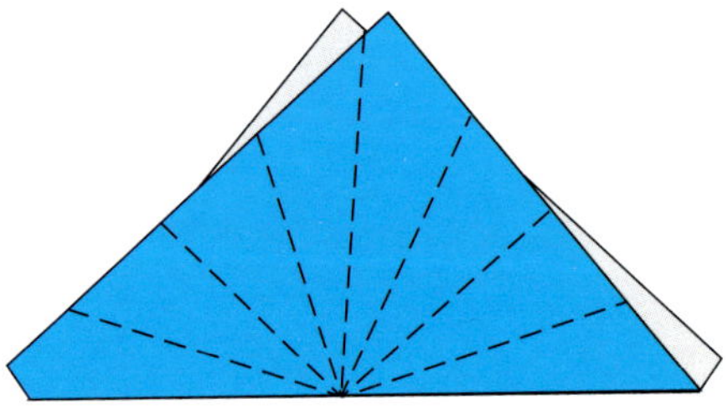

2 Fold and then unfold along all the dotted lines one by one.

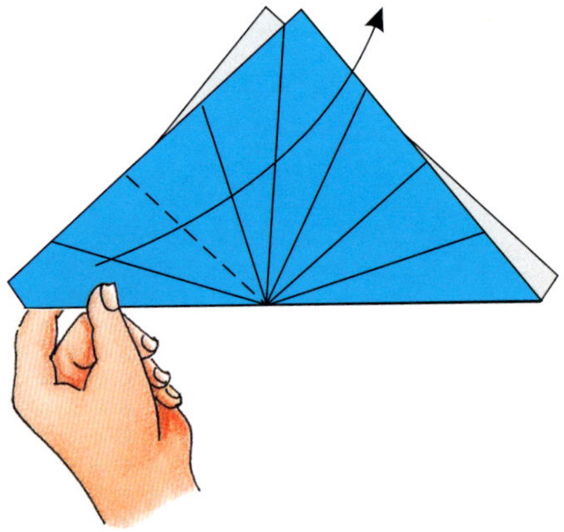

3 Fold up the left corner along the dotted line as shown.

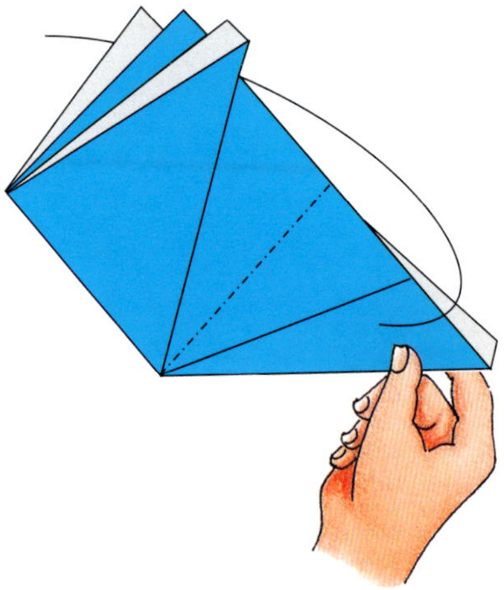

4 Bring the right corner up from the back along the dotted line.

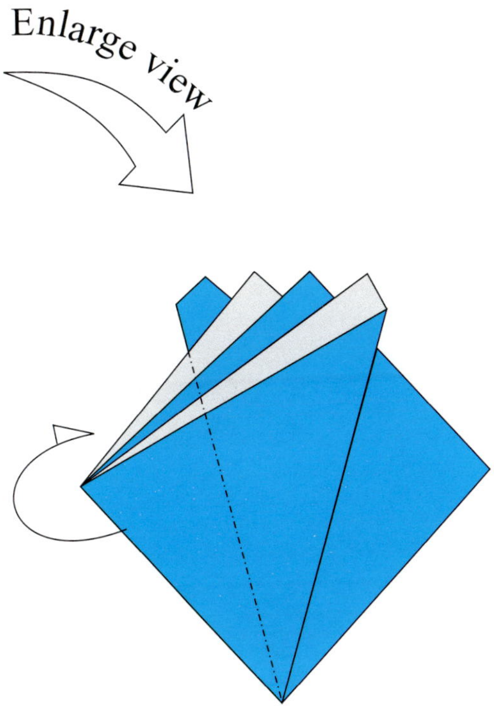

5 Fold the left corner towards its back along the dotted line as shown.

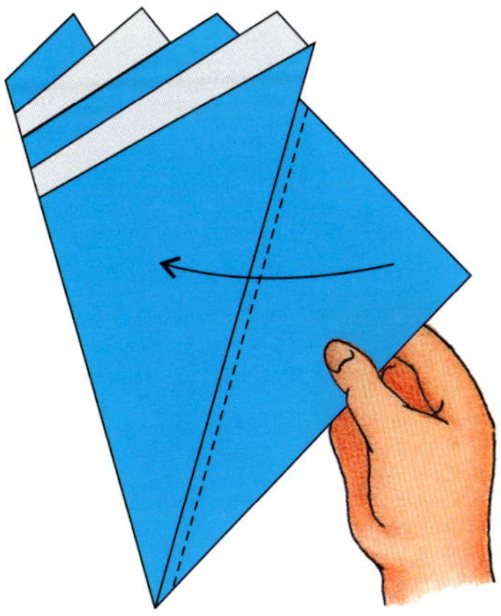

6 Fold the right corner towards left.

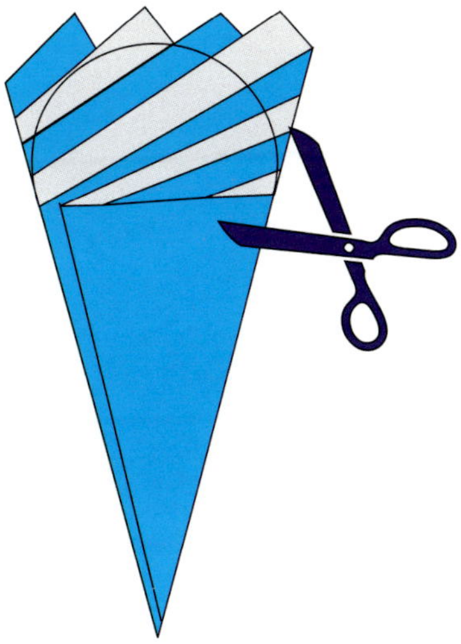

7 Cut the upper edges round to form the shape of a softy....

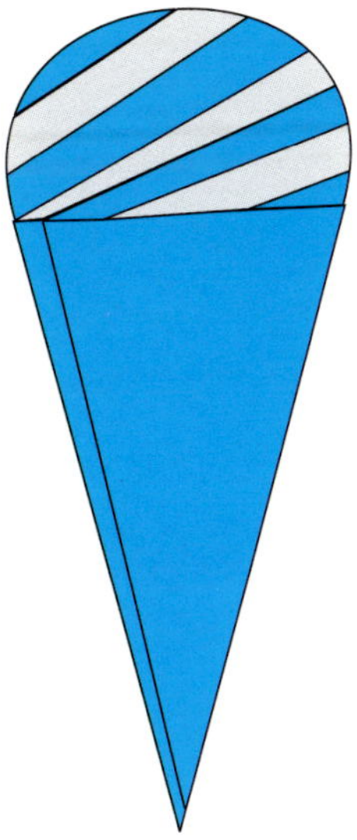

8 .... like this.

Crow

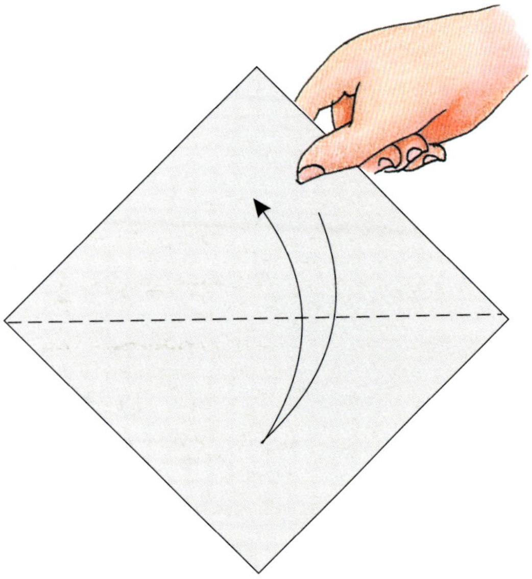

1 Make a centre crease and unfold it.

2 Fold both the top and bottom corners to the centre crease.

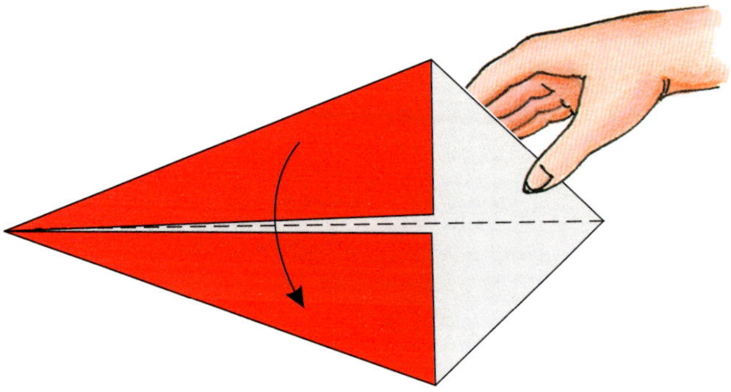

3 Fold the form in half bringing the top corner to meet the bottom.

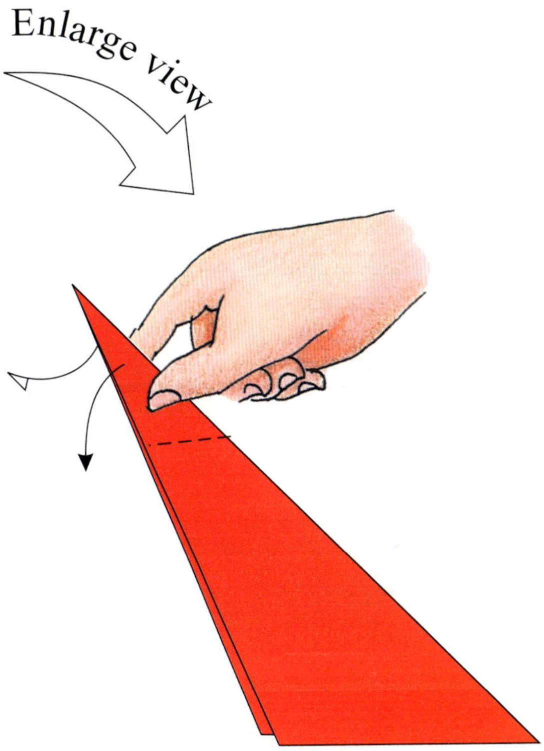

4 To make a pocket fold, fold backward and forward along the dotted line....

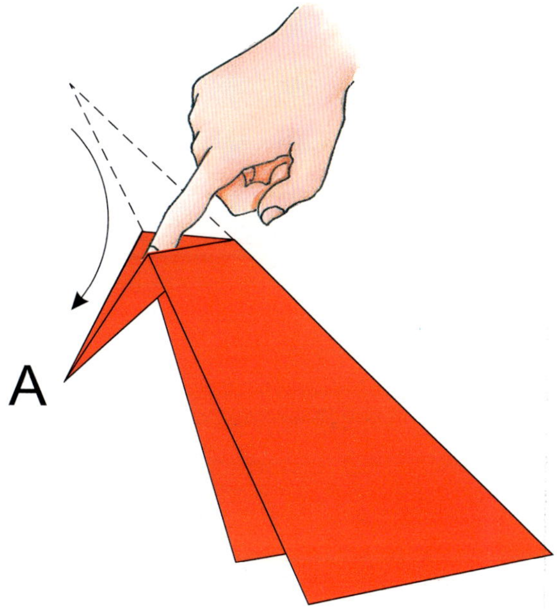

6 Open up the form slightly and thrust the point "A" inside to make the beak of the crow.

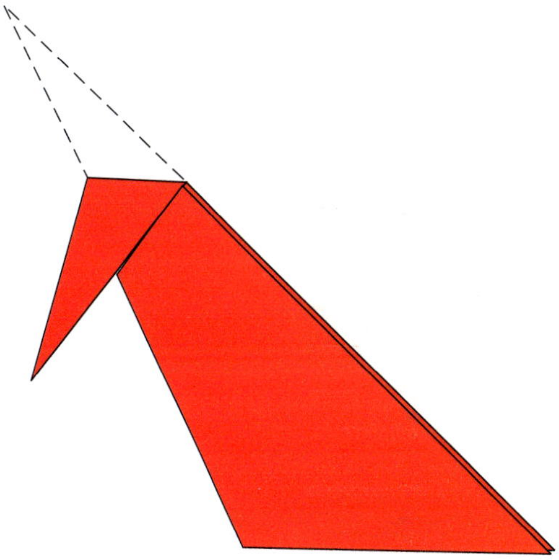

5 .... like this and unfold it.

7 Paste paper feathers to it. Draw eyes and it's ready to fly.

Dog

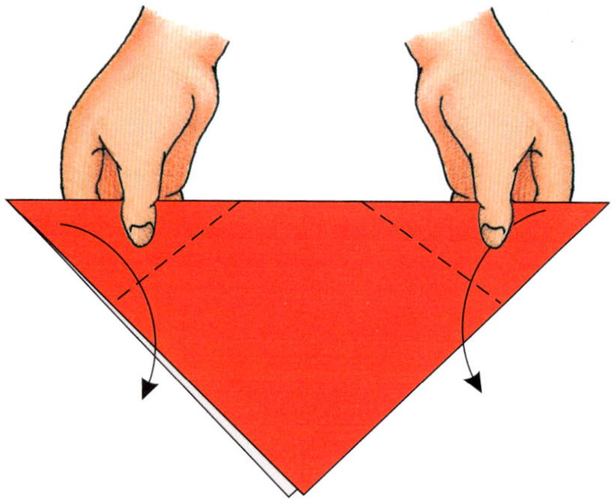

2 Fold in the direction of arrows as shown to form the dog's ears.

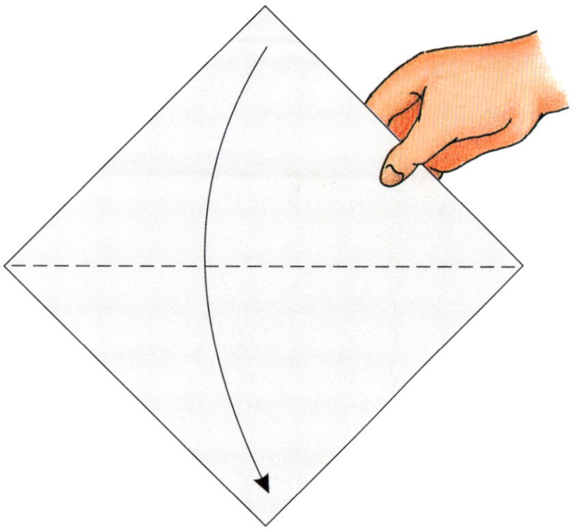

1 Use quarter sheet of a paper. Make a centre crease and fold.

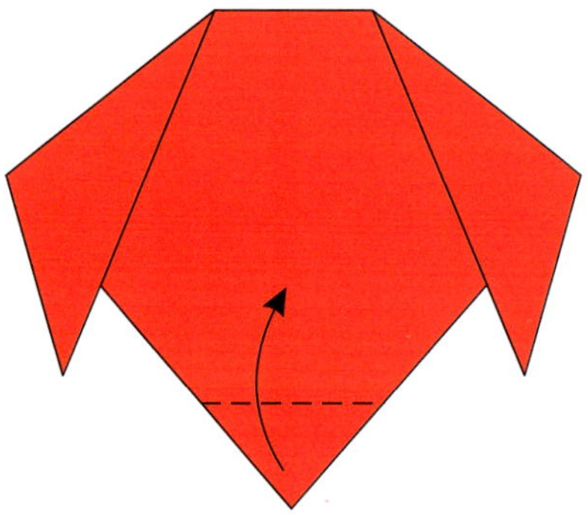

3 Fold the lower end of the front layer upwards along the dotted line.

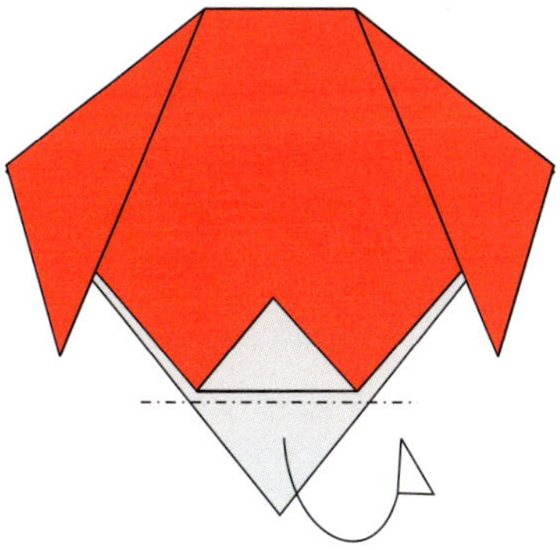

4 Fold the lower end of the back layer backwards along the dotted line.

5 Draw eyes and nose.

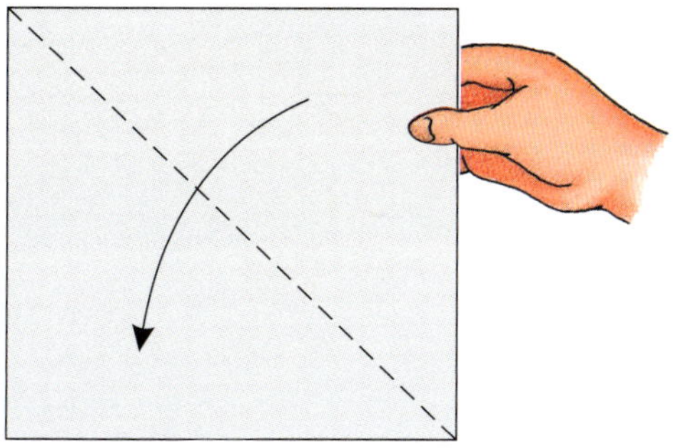

6 Use another sheet. Make the centre crease and fold.

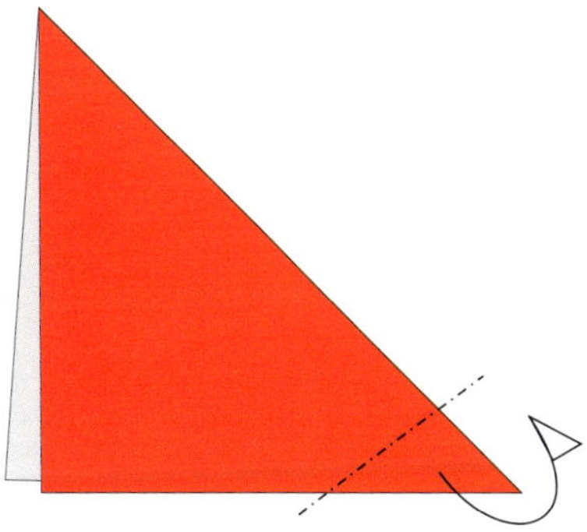

7 Turn the lower right corner backward....

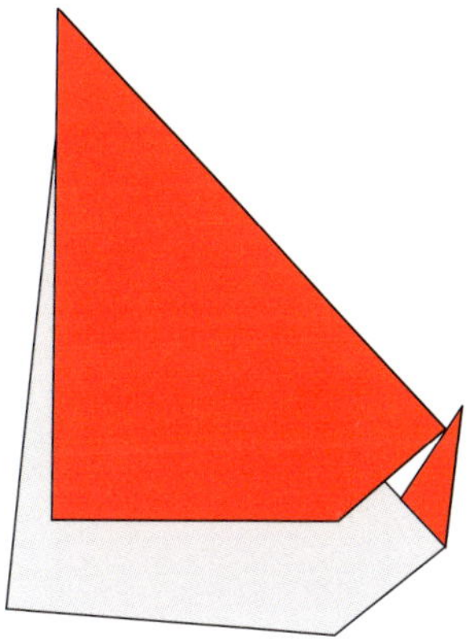

8 ...like this.

9 Paste the head as shown, and your dog is ready.

Lantern

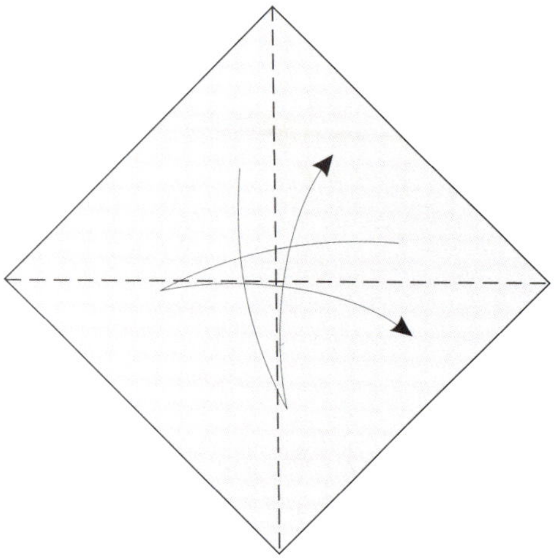

1 Fold then unfold along the dotted lines.

2 Fold all the four corners to the centre.

3 Again fold the four corners to the centre.

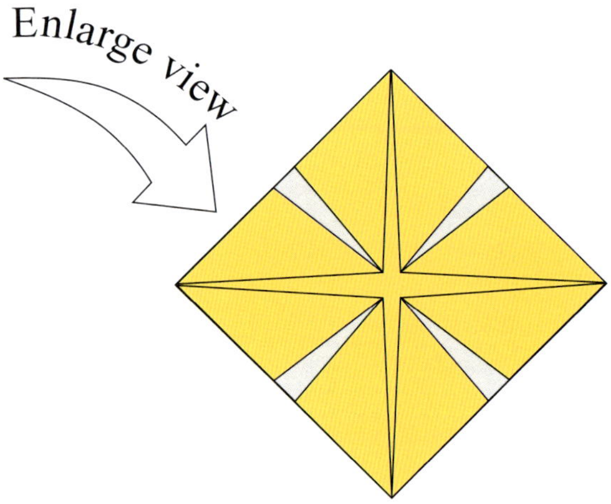

4 Your form will look like this.

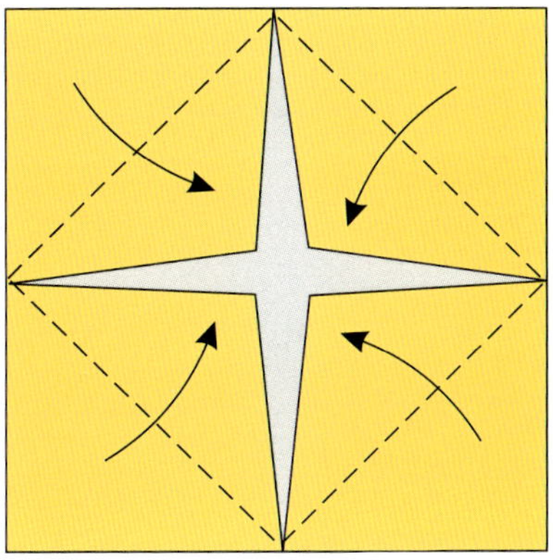

5 Fold all the four corners to the centre.

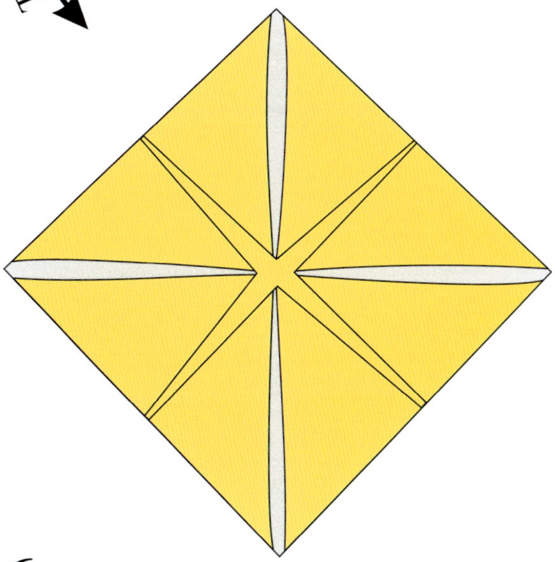

6 Your form will look like this.

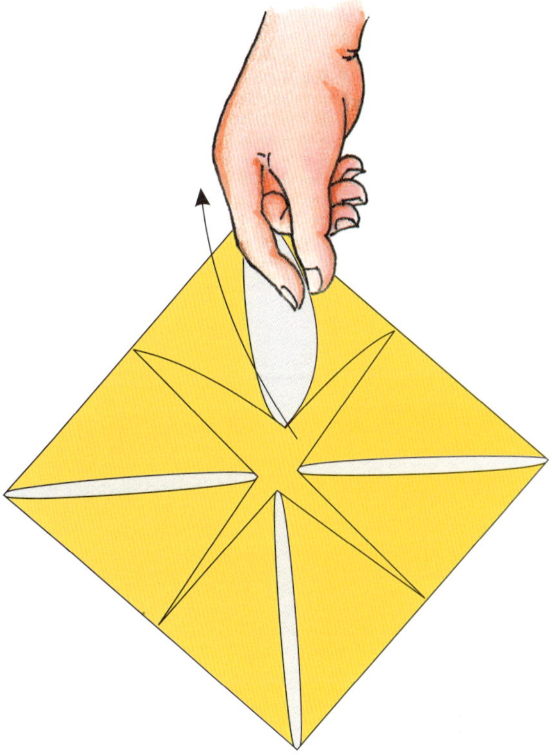

7 Open a square and flatten it to form a rectangle. Repeat the process for the opposite square.

8 Now your lantern is ready.

Holiday Basket

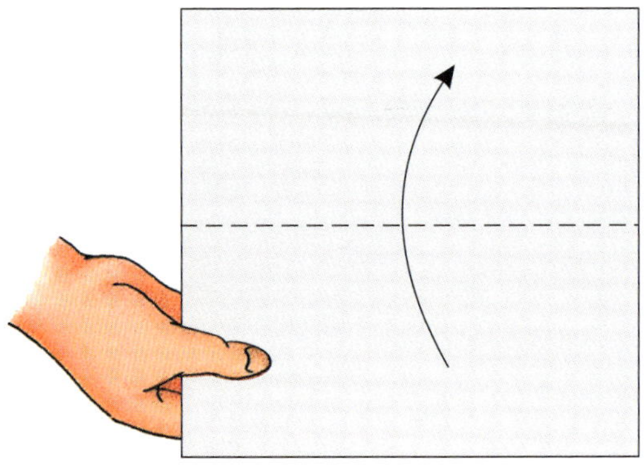

1 Fold the paper in half along the dotted line.

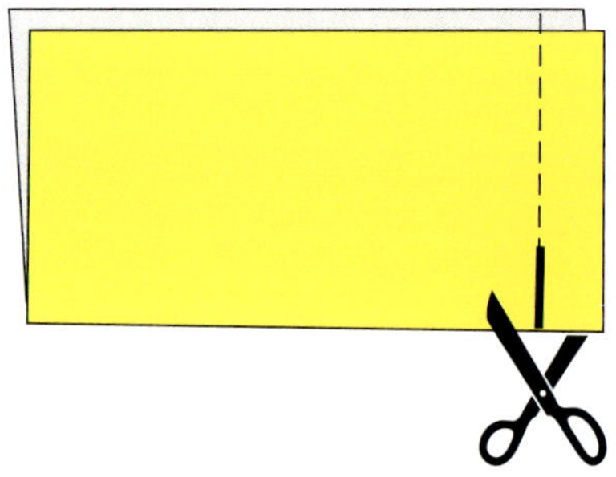

2 Cut along the dotted line, half inch from the right edge.

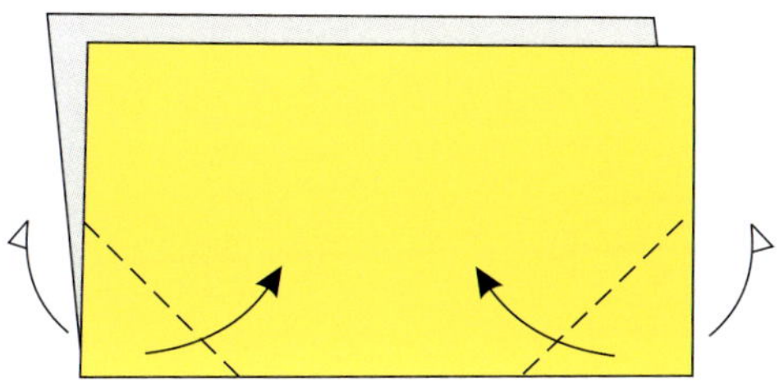

3 Fold both the corners forward and backward.

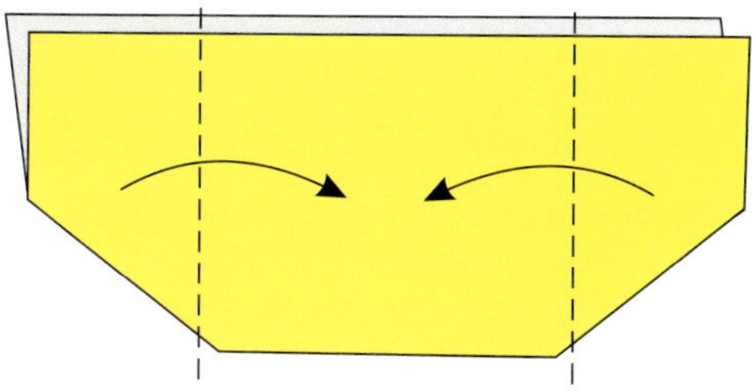

4 Tuck both the corners inside the form.

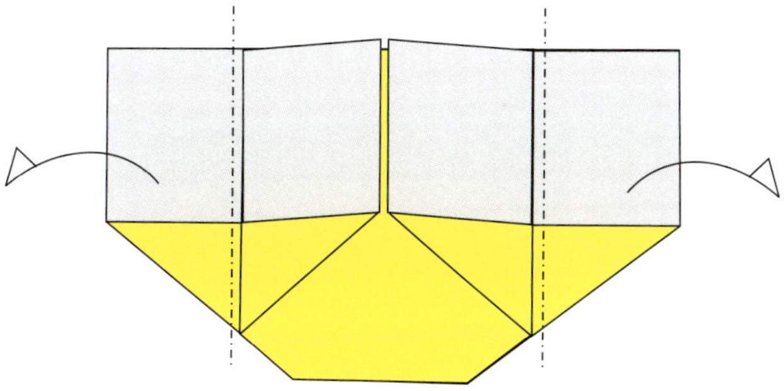

5 Fold both the sides of the upper flaps to meet the centre line.
Repeat same steps with the back flap.

6 Fold the front side twice inside, so that the second fold is tucked into the basket.

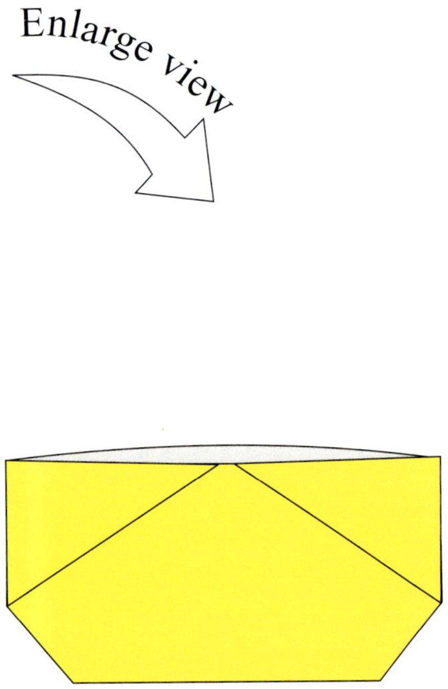

7 Repeat the same step with the back flap, so the shape of the basket will be like this.

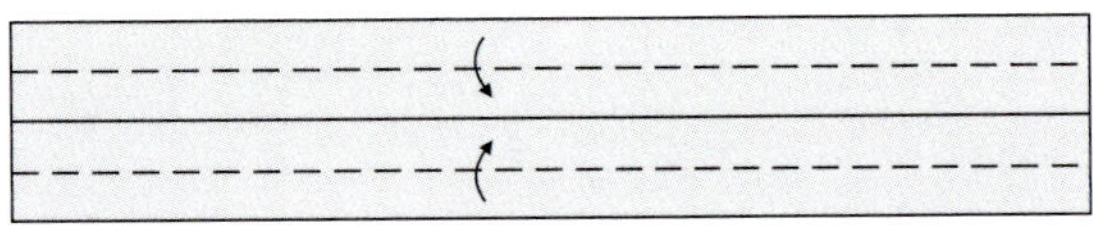

8 Now pick the paper strip which you get from the step number 2, and fold in half as shown.

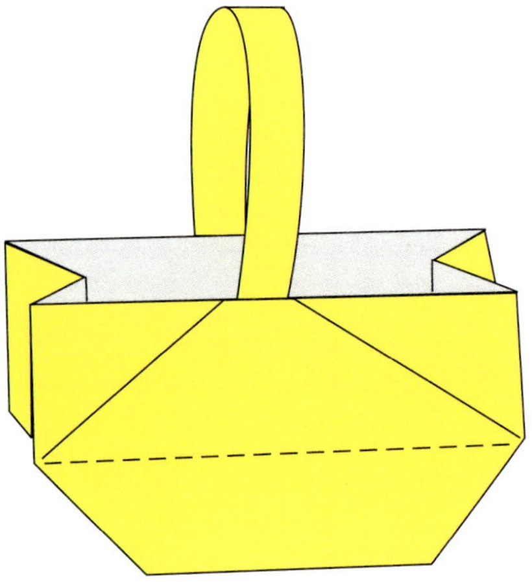

9 Paste both ends of the strip to the sides of your basket. Make a sharp crease across the bottom.

10 Open the basket and flatten it at the base. Your holiday basket is ready.

Collage Work

Holiday Basket

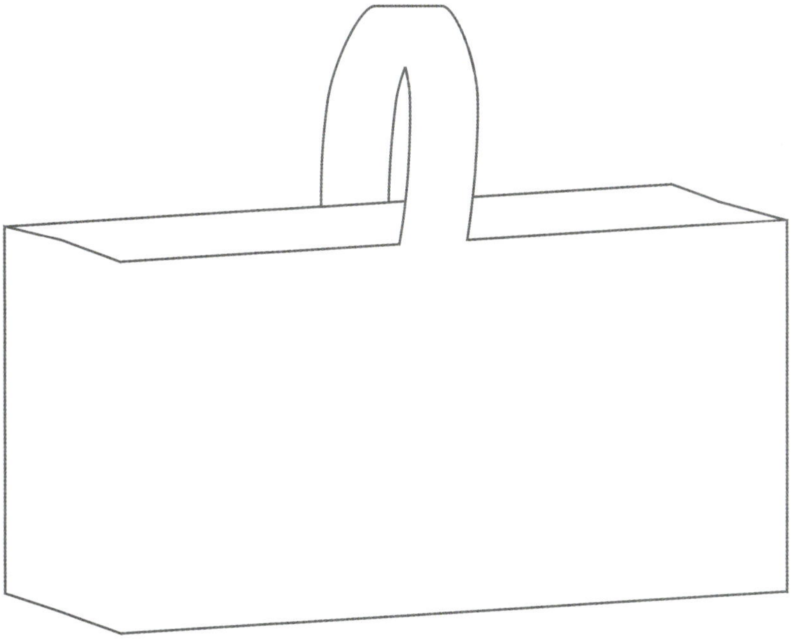

TIPS AND TRICKS

Step-1 Collect paper sheets of various colours of your own choice. Tear them in small pieces of different shapes.

Step-2 Set them within the outline and paste in the given shape.

Cut and Paste

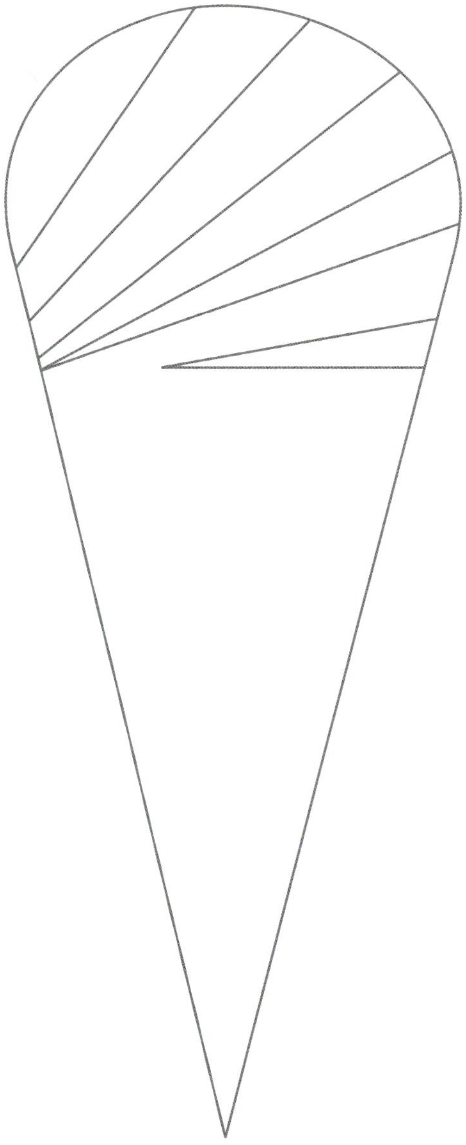

Softy

TIPS AND TRICKS

Step-1 Take craft paper sheets of various colours. Trace different parts on the shape of different colours.

Step-2 Now paste these pieces at the appropriate places.

Crushed Paper Art

Crow

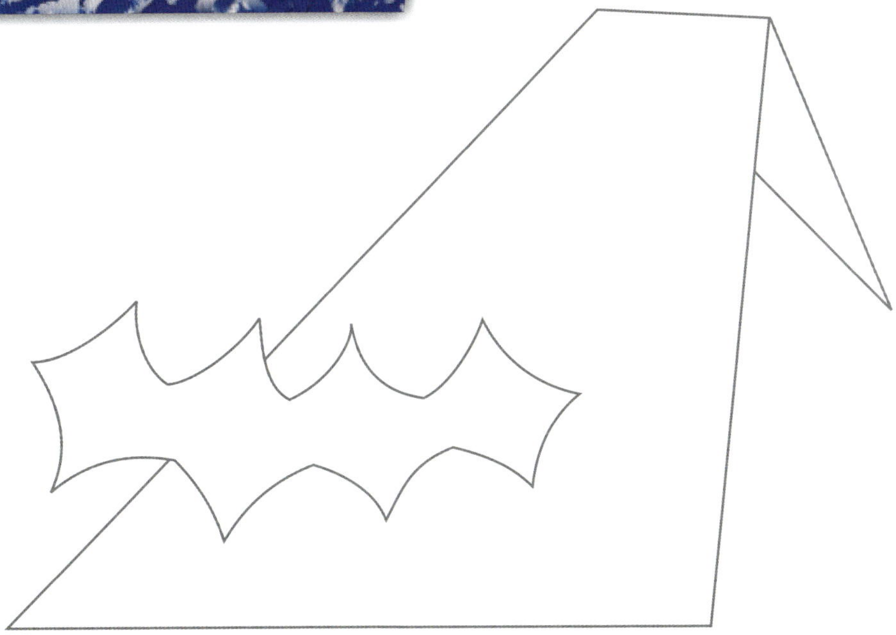

TIPS AND TRICKS

Step-1 Take a plain paper and squeeze it in your hand. Open it gently and apply the poster colour with a flat brush.

Step-2 Now cut the paper according to the shape and paste it within the outline.

Spray Paint

Fox Head

TIPS AND TRICKS

Step-1
Take a white paper. Spray different colours of your own choice with a tooth brush on the white paper.

Step-2
Cut the parts of the shape as per your liking and paste them on the figure.

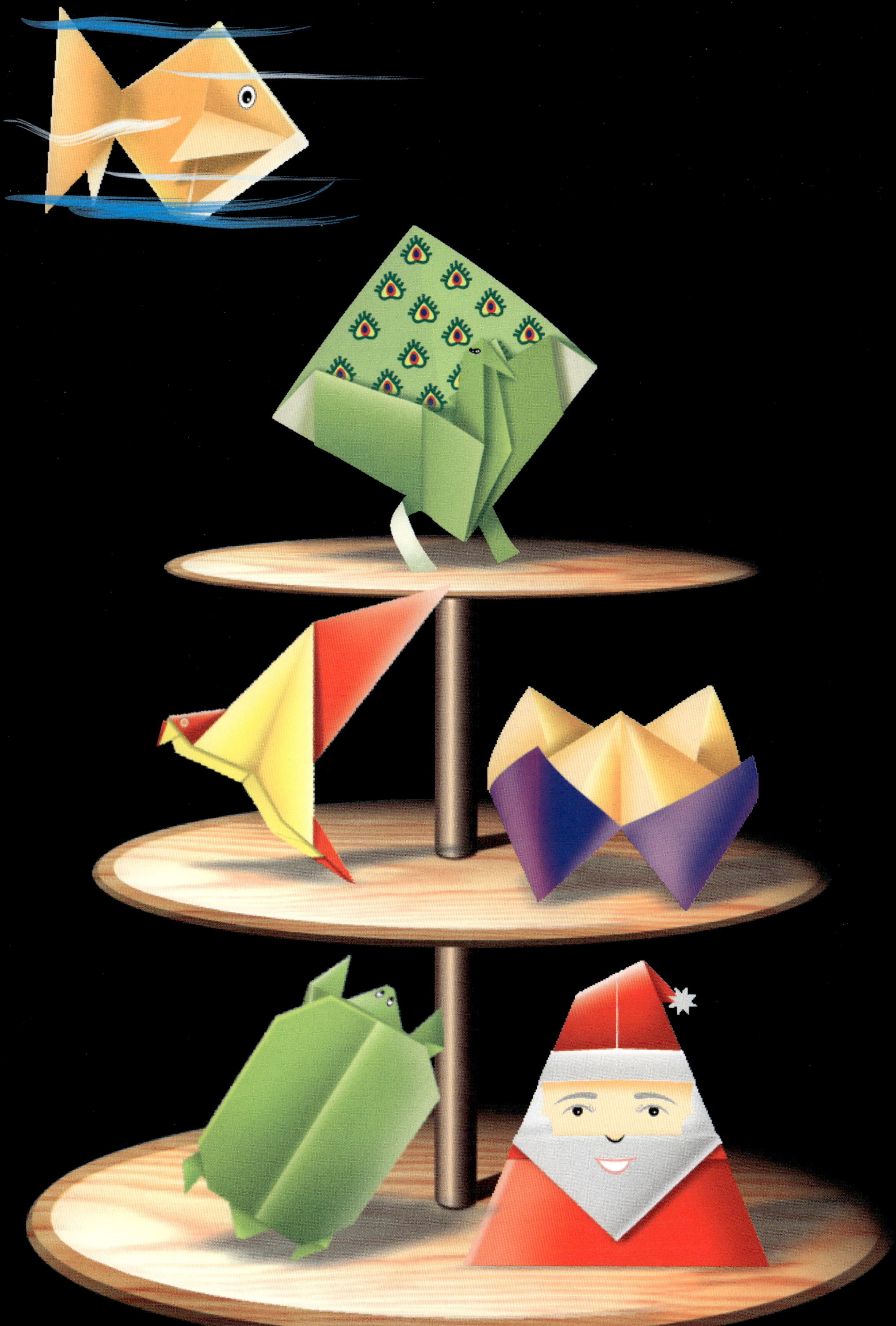

Peacock

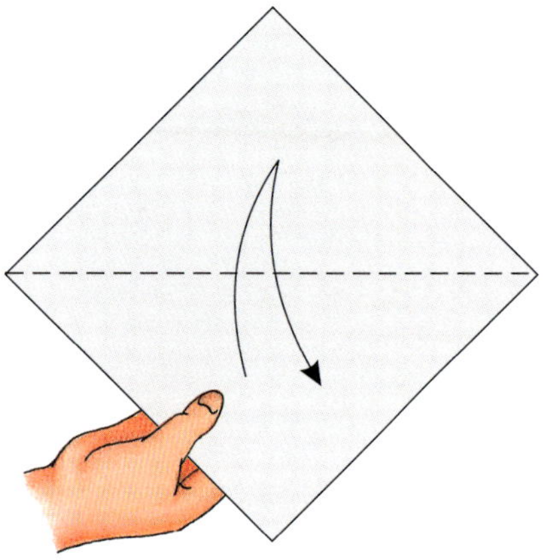

1 Fold the paper in half and unfold it.

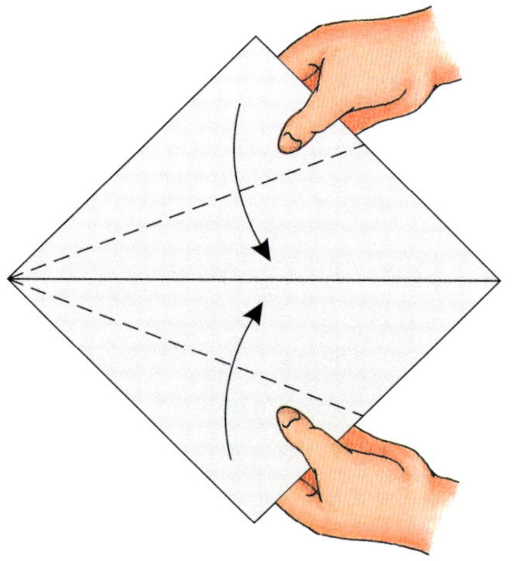

2 Fold the top and the bottom corners along the dotted lines.

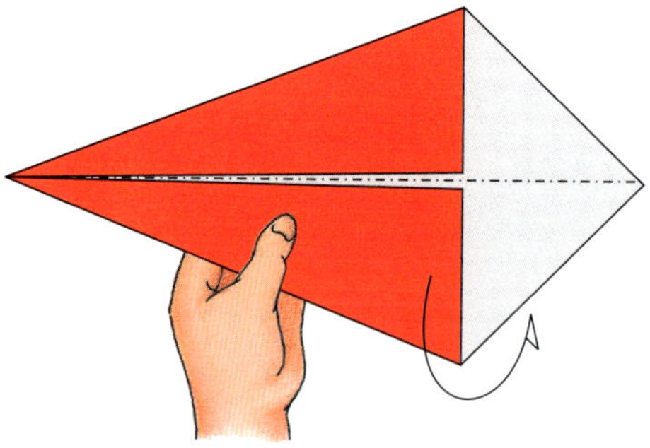

3 Fold backwards in half along the dotted line.

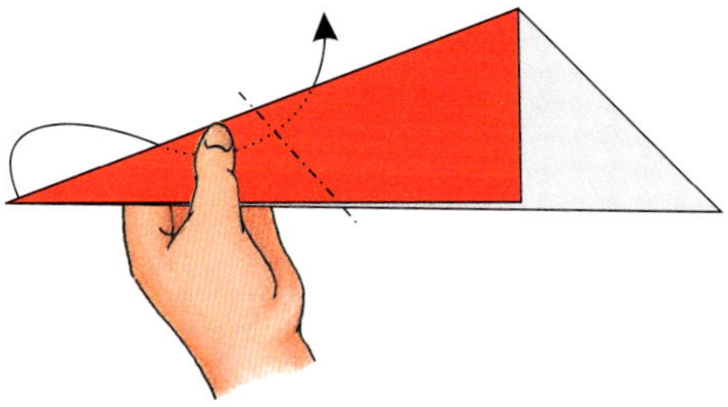

4 Make a pocket fold to form the bird's neck.

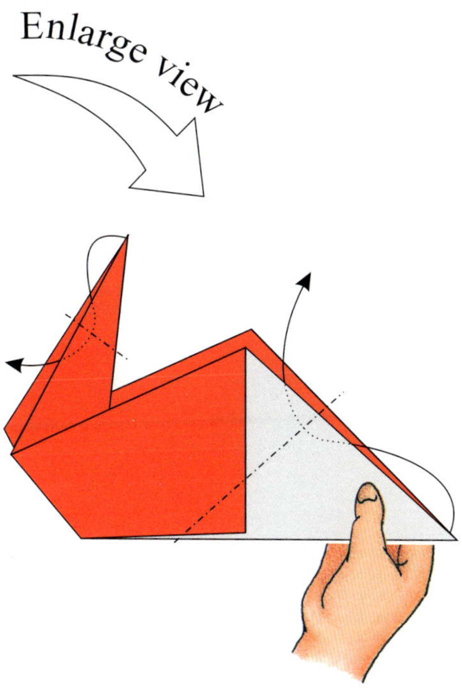

5 Again make a pocket fold at the left side for the head. Make another pocket fold at the right side for the tail.

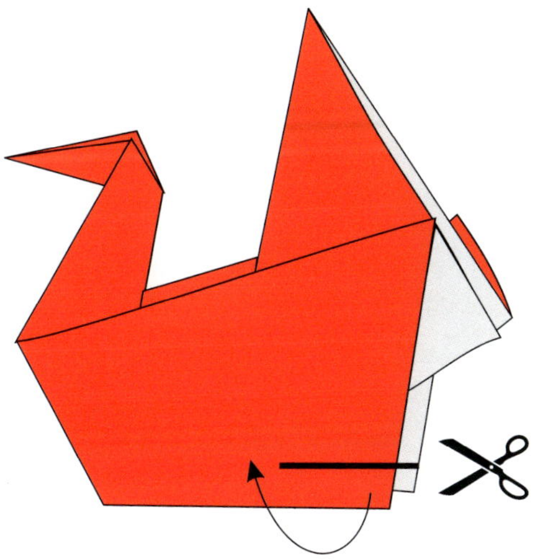

6 Make a cut and fold the flaps to form the legs.

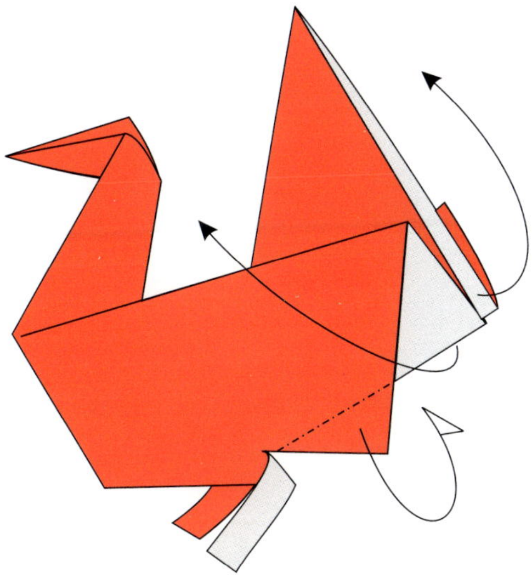

7 Fold the right-side bottom corners inside and spread out the tail.

8 Draw colourful feather spots to complete the peacock.

Goldfish

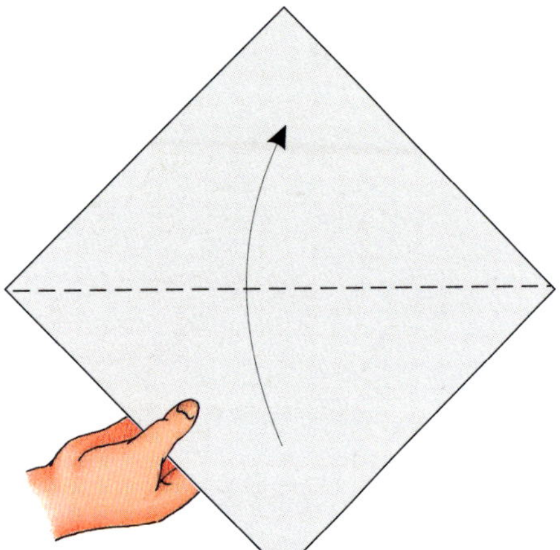

1 Fold in half.

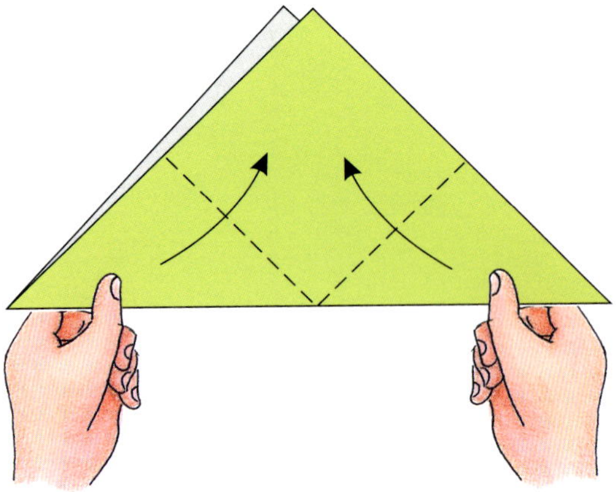

2 Fold both the side corners up to meet at the top centre.

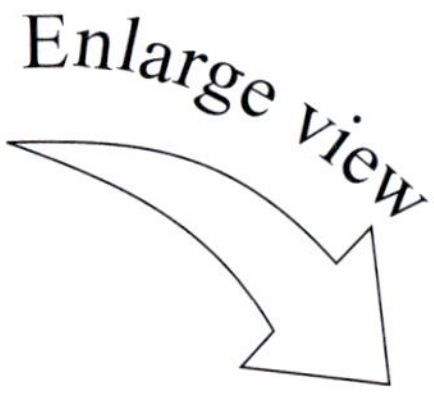

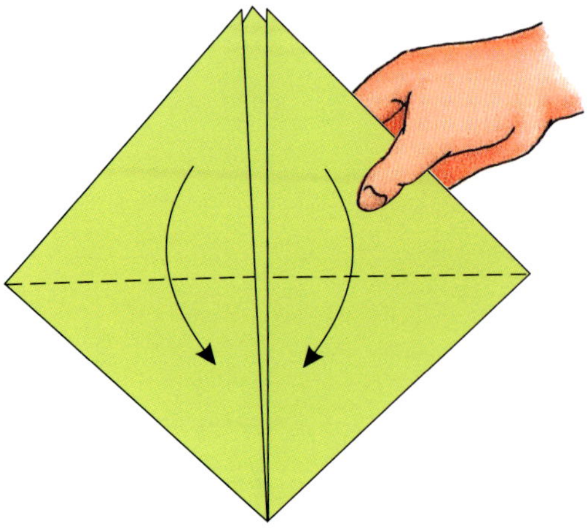

3 Fold the upper flaps downward.

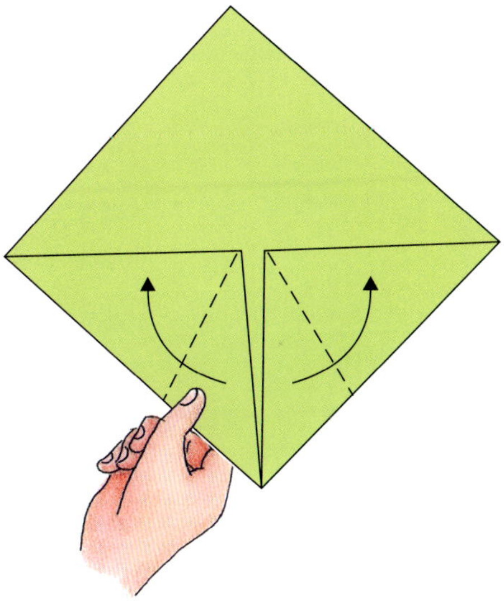

4 Fold both the flaps outwards along the dotted lines....

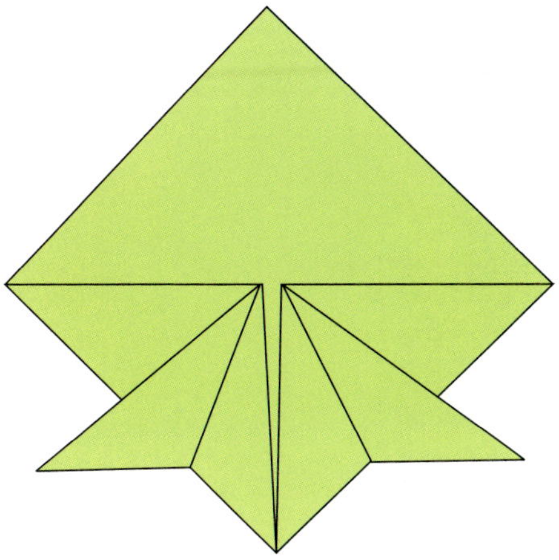

5 ....like this

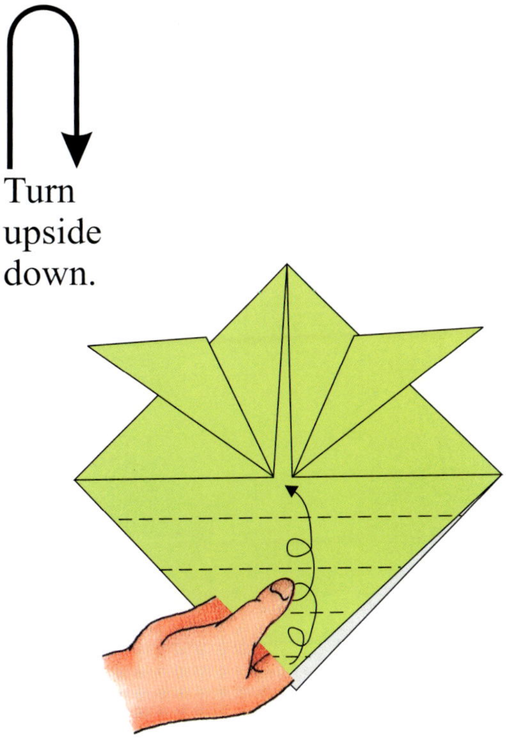

6 Fold the upper flap upwards as shown.

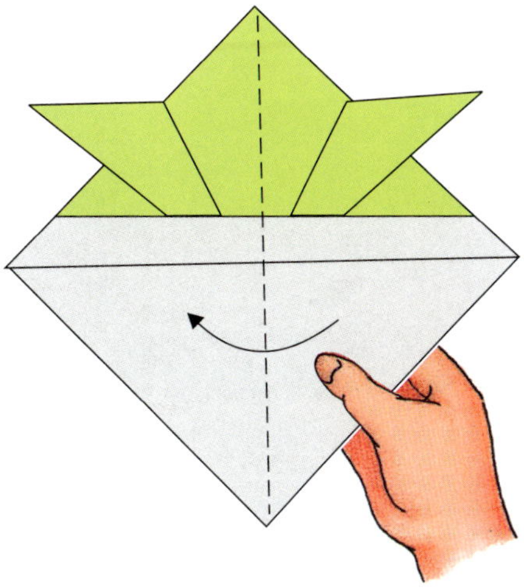

7 Fold the form in half in the direction of arrow.

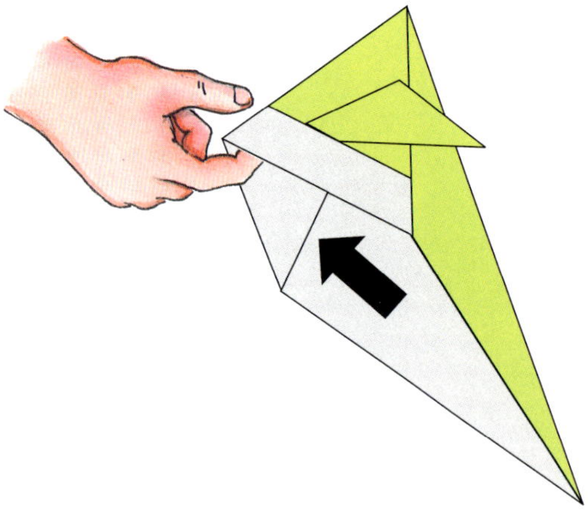

8 Now pull the top face of the form out by inserting your finger in it.

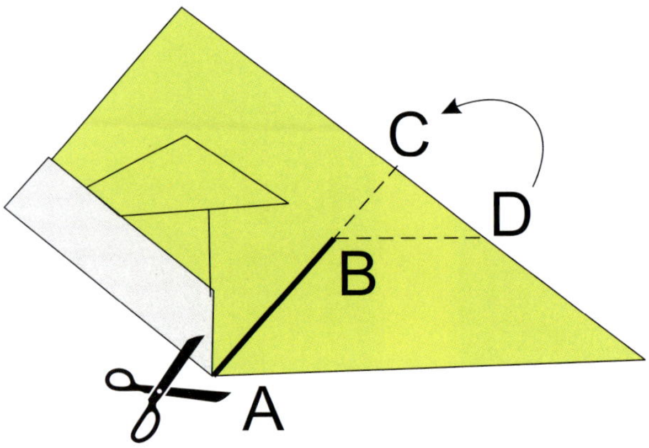

9 Cut the marked portion from 'A' to 'B'. Make the tail by putting point 'D' over 'C'.

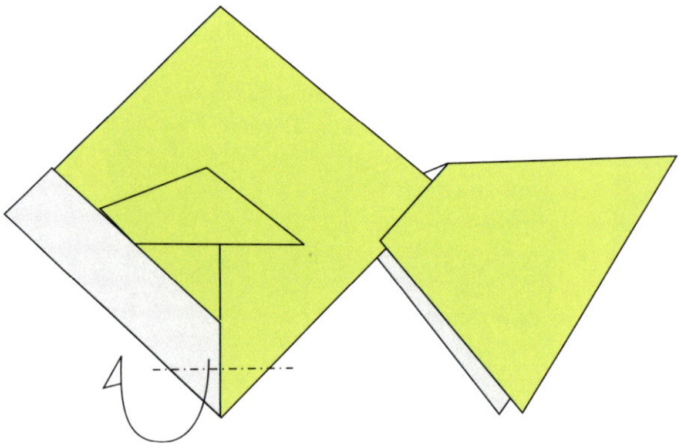

10 Fold and paste the bottom corner to form a ring.

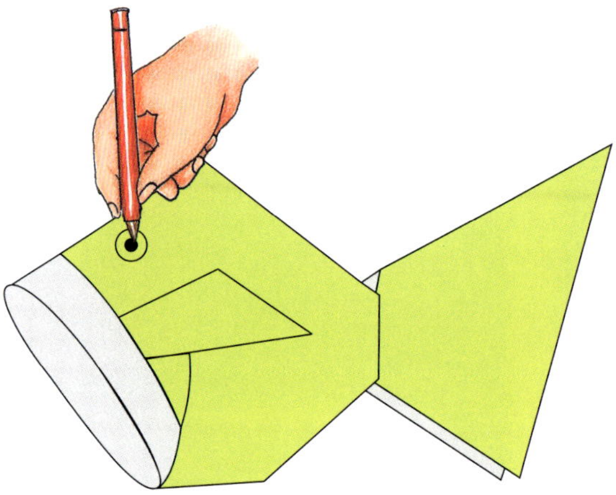

11 Draw the eyes and your goldfish is ready to swim.

Santa Claus

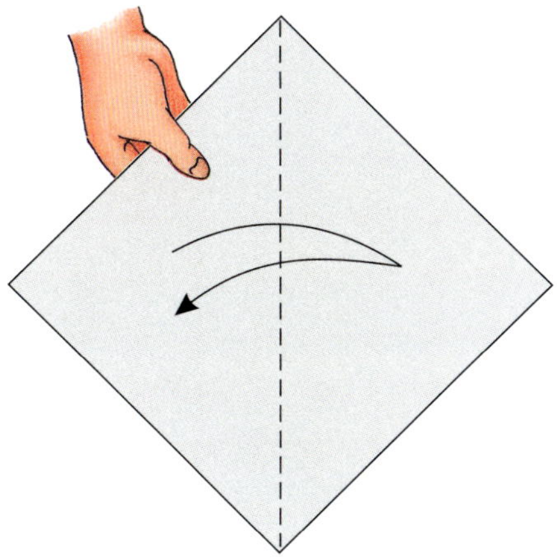

1 Spread paper after making centre crease.

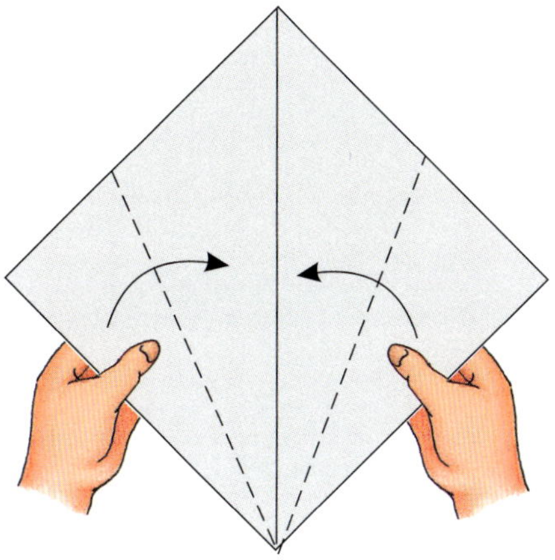

2 Fold along the dotted lines....

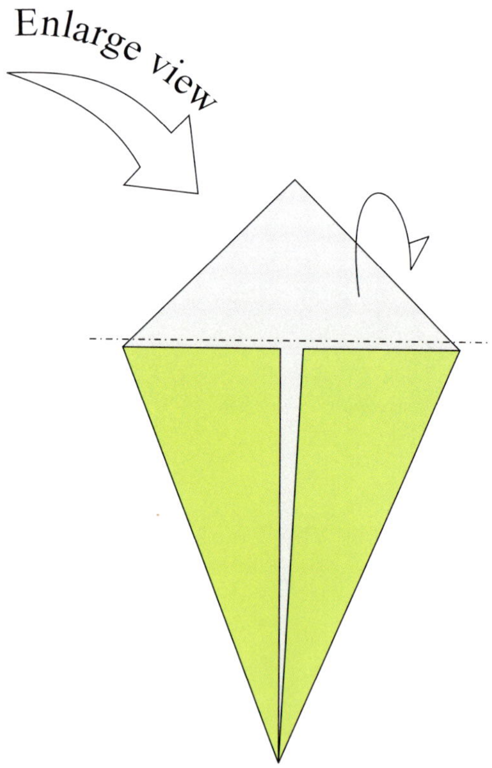

3 ...like this.
Fold the top flap behind.

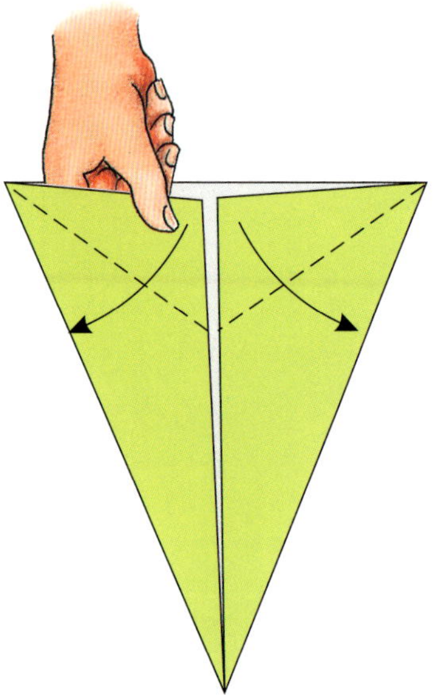

4 Fold both the top flaps downwards along the dotted lines.

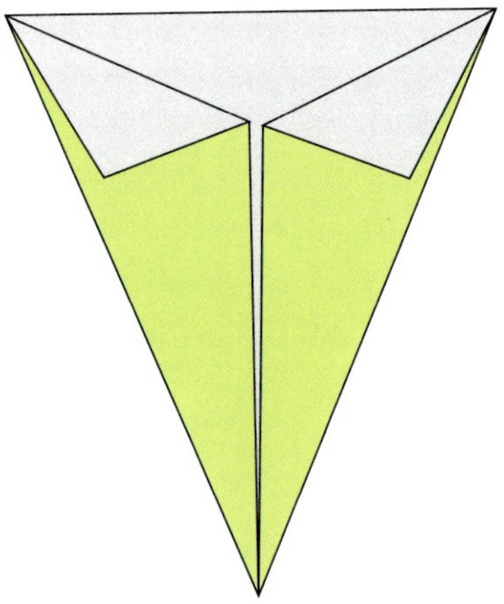

5 Your form will be like this.

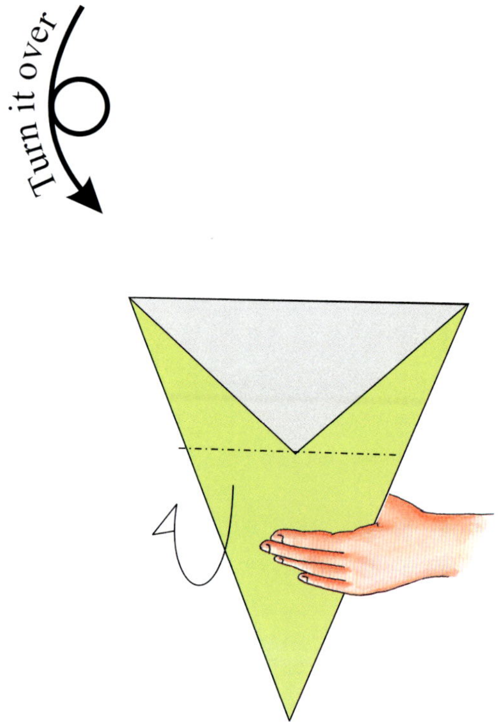

6 Fold the lower flap backwards along the dotted line.

Enlarge view

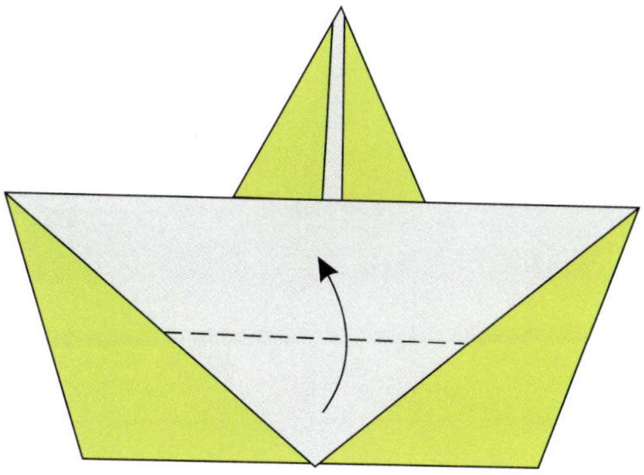

7 Now fold along the dotted line in the direction of arrow.

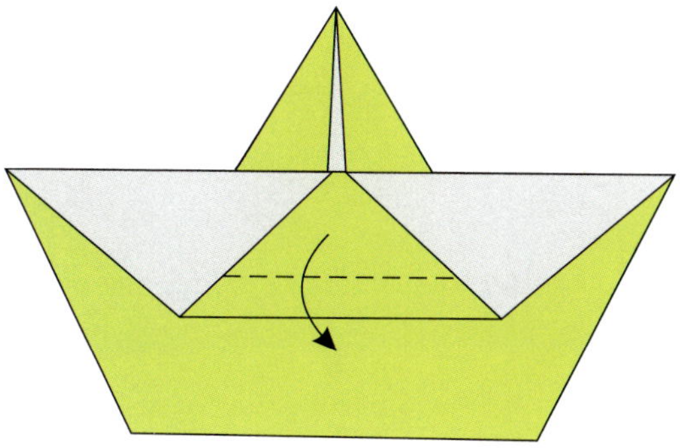

8 Again fold downwards.

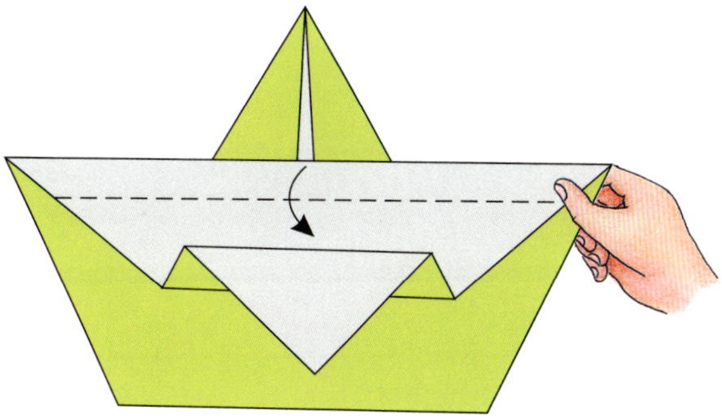

9 Fold the upper side in the direction of arrow.

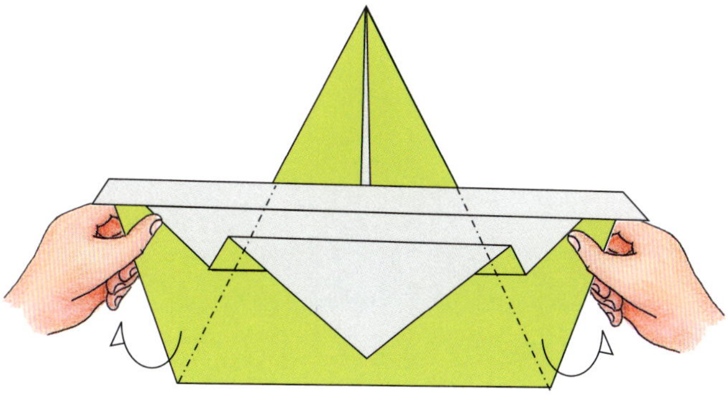

10 Fold the right and left sides behind the form along the dotted lines.

11 Fold the top flaps backward along the dotted line.

12 Paste a paper ball at the tip of cap.

13 Draw santa's face on it.

14 The santa is ready to give you the Christmas gift.

Tortoise

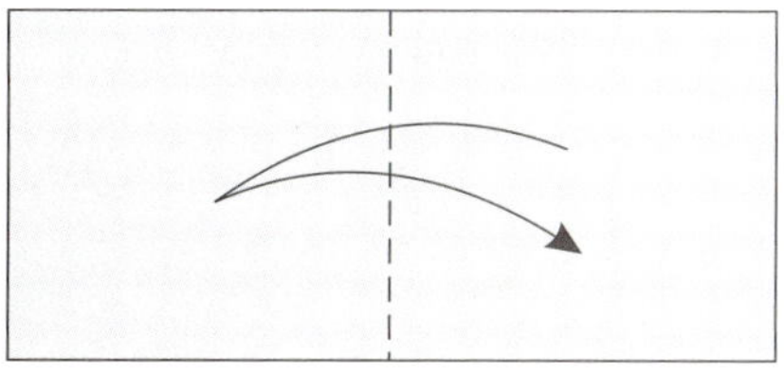

1 Take half sheet of the paper.
Make a centre crease then unfold.

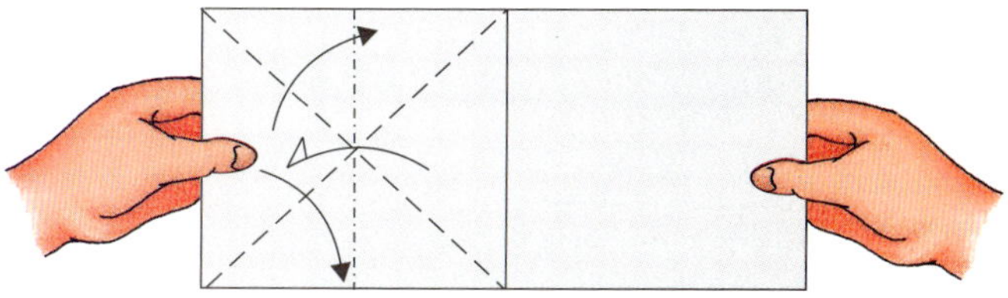

2 Make all the three folds on the left side in the direction of arrows, and then unfold.

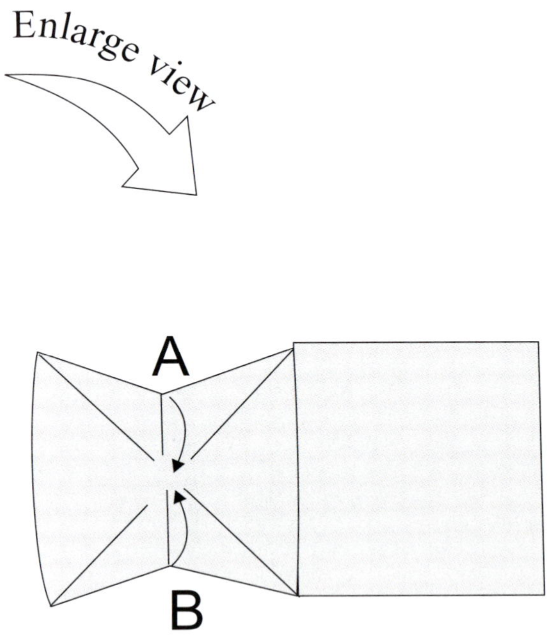

3 Make points 'A' and 'B' touch each other by folding the paper in the direction of arrows.

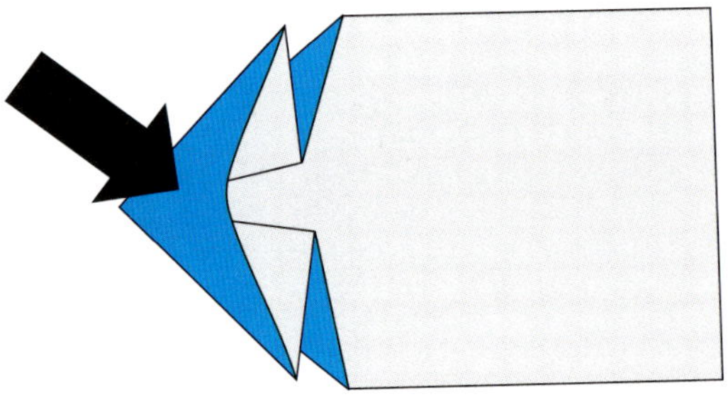

4 Now press the top triangular flap to fatten it.

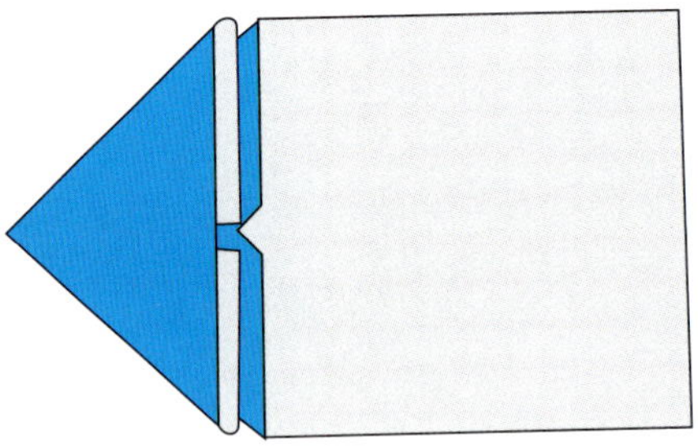

5 Your form will look like this. Fold the right side in the same way.

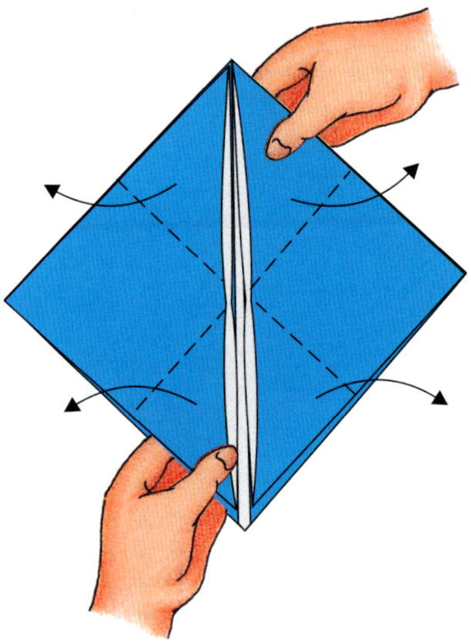

6 Fold all the four flaps along the dotted lines.

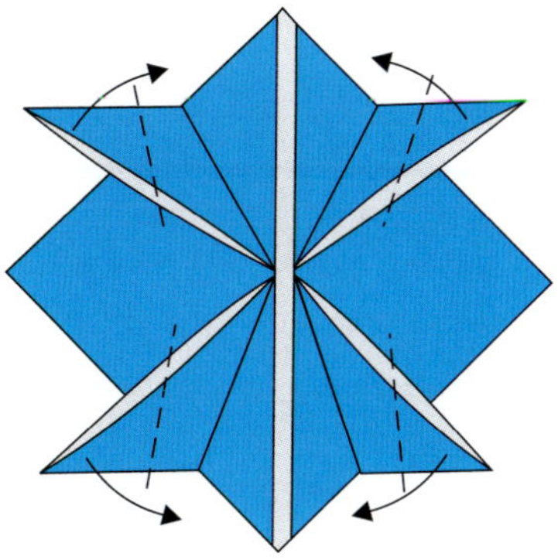

7 Again fold all the four flaps in the direction of arrows.

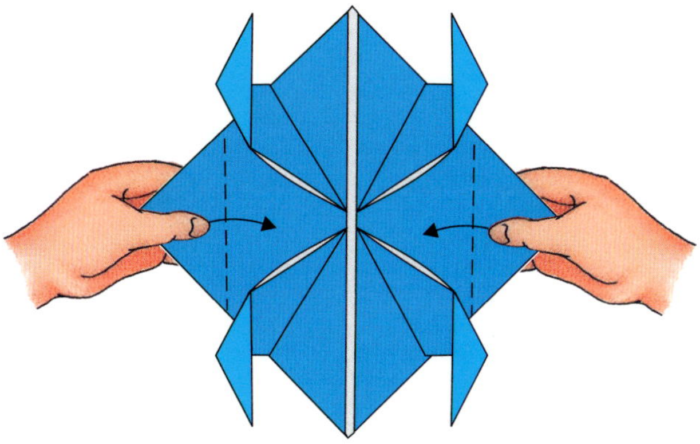

8 Fold both the right and left corners inside.

9 Make stair-step folds at the top and bottom corners as shown.

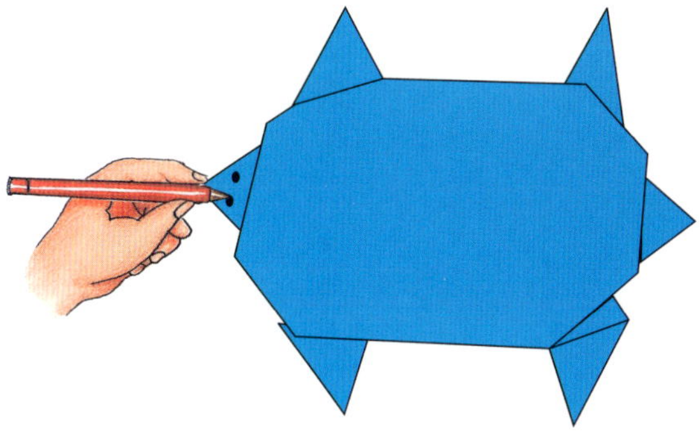

10 Draw eyes and your tortoise is ready to crawl.

Pigeon

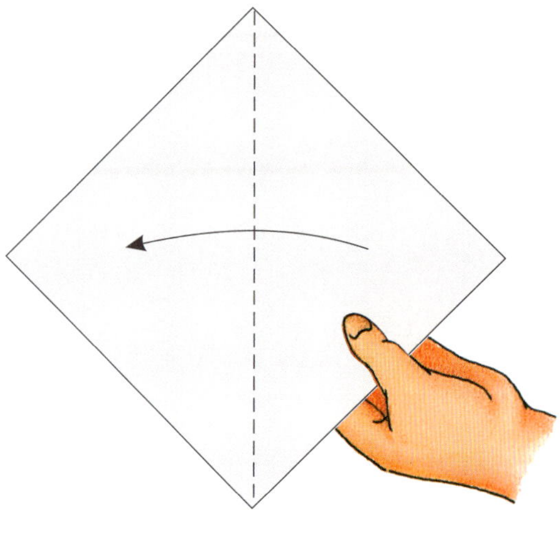

1 Fold in half along the dotted line.

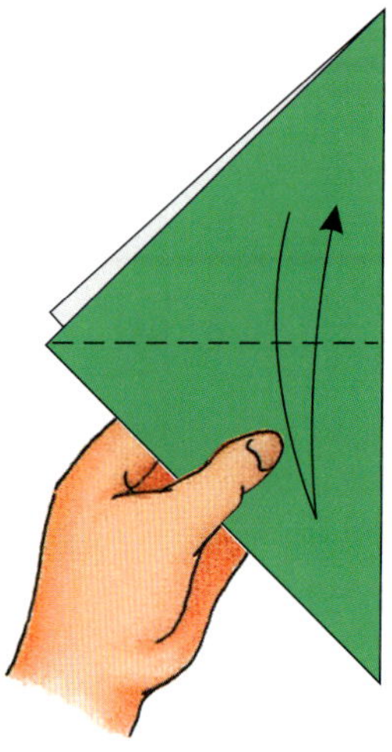

2 Fold and unfold along the dotted line.

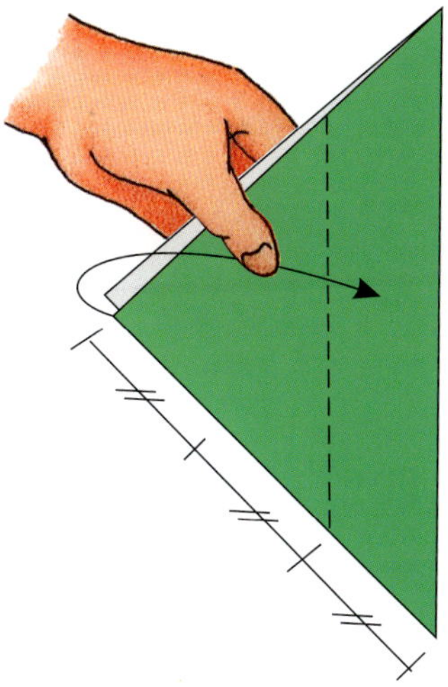

3 Fold both the flaps to right from the appropriate point.

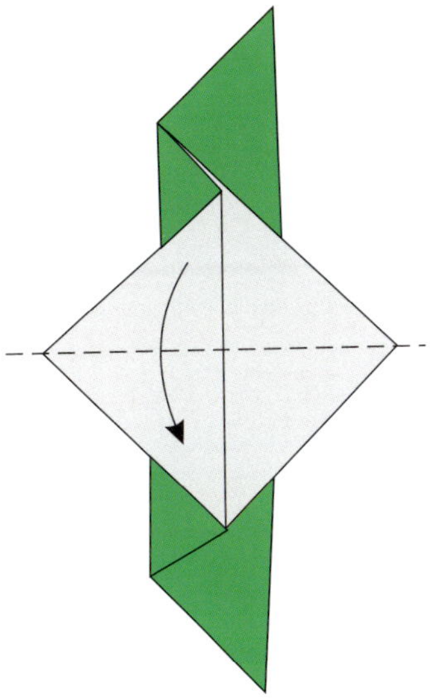

5 Fold the form in half.

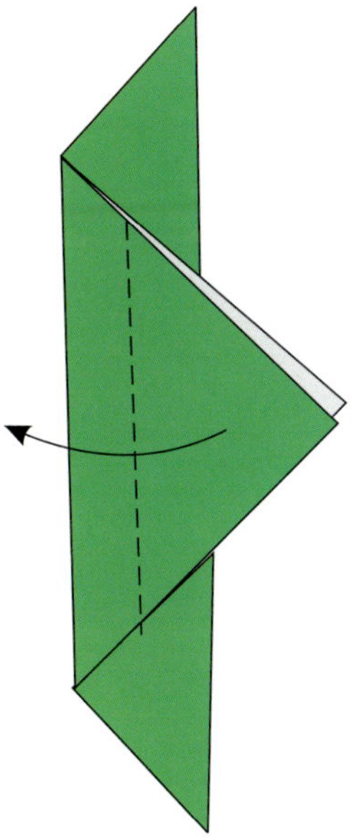

4 Make the upper flap open along the dotted line.

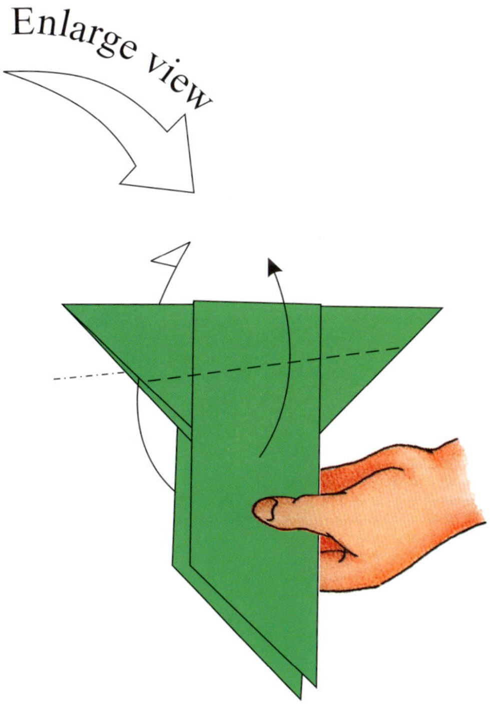

6 Fold both the lower flaps upward.

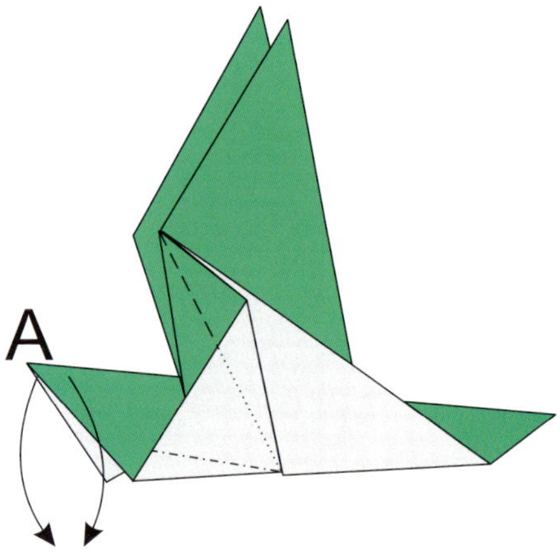

7 Put the point 'A' in fingers and stretch it to maximum downward position. Make crease along the new position of the wings as shown along the dotted lines.

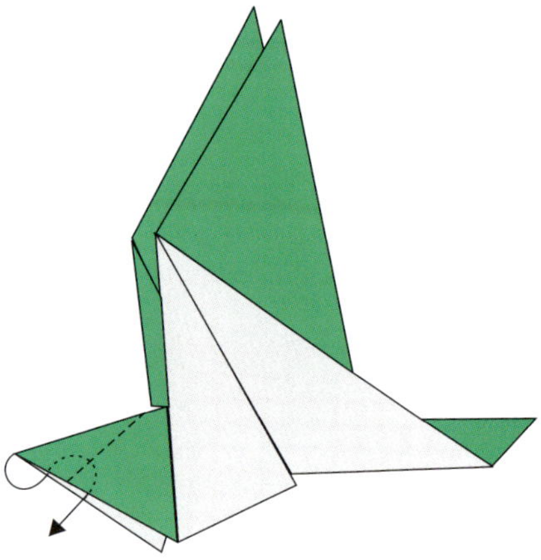

8 Make a pocket fold along the dotted line.

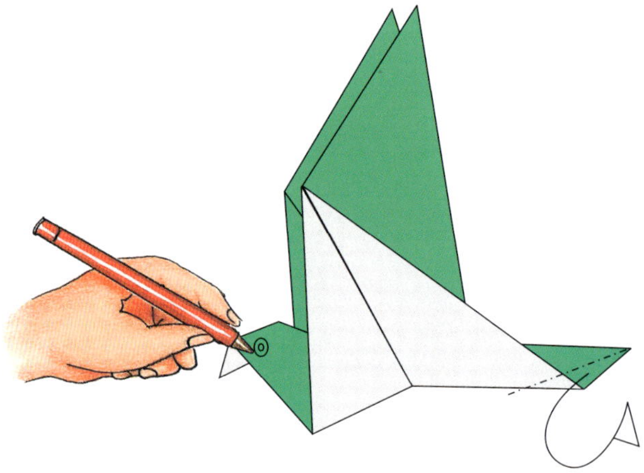

9 Fold both the bottom corners inside and draw eyes and your bird is ready.

10 Hold as shown pushing and pulling makes wings go up and down.

Candy Box

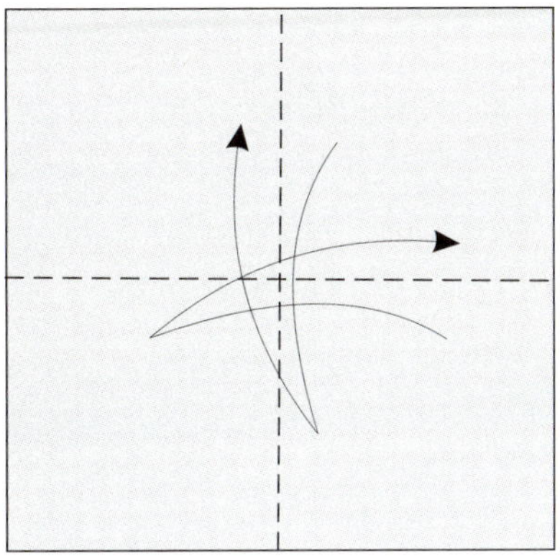

1 Fold and unfold along both the dotted lines.

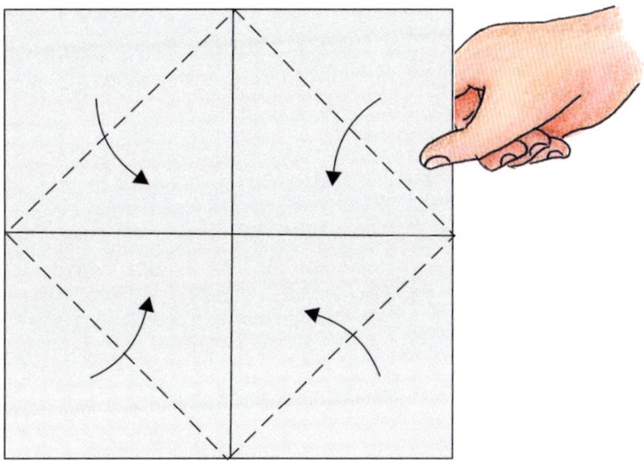

2 Fold all the four corners inside to the centre point....

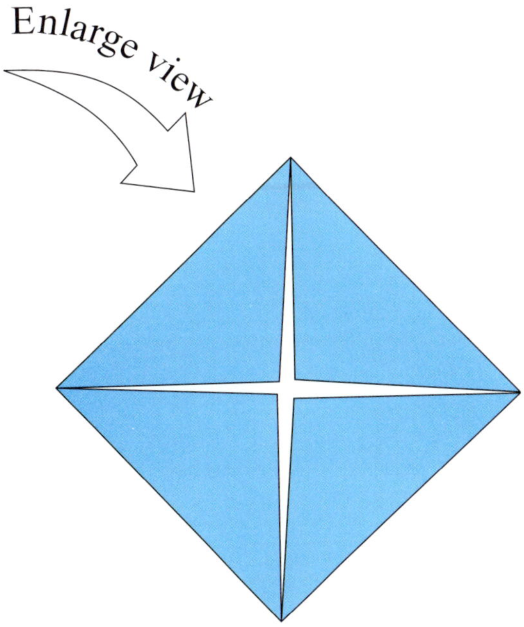

3 ....like this.

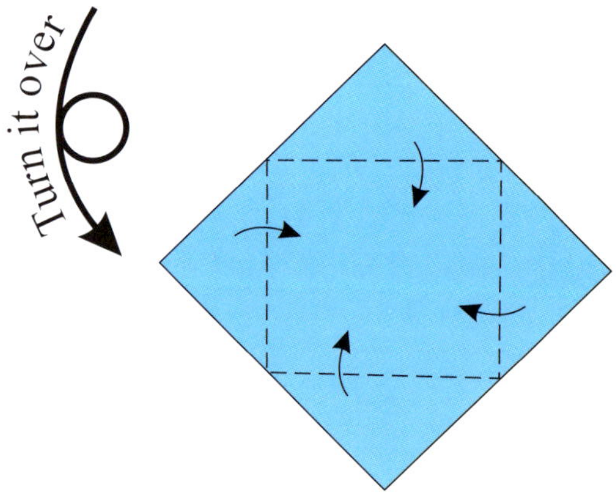

4 Fold inwards along all the four dotted lines.

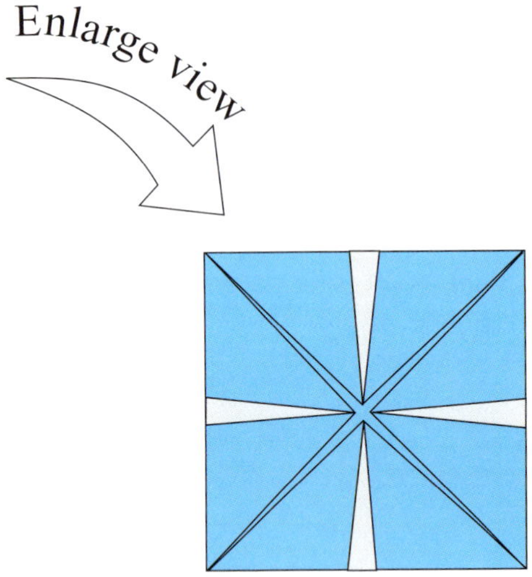

5 Your shape of the form will look like this.

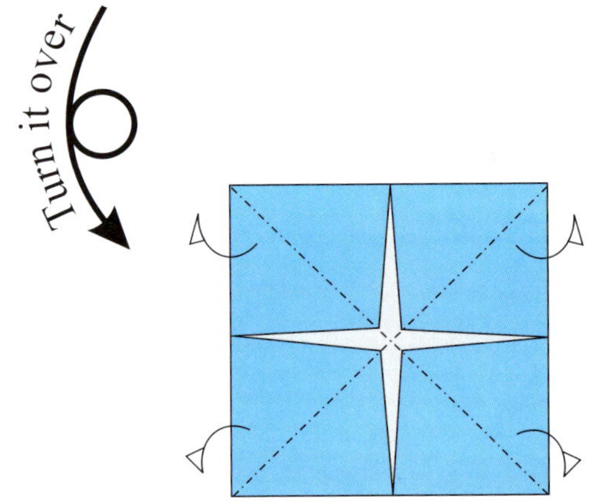

6 Fold backwards along the dotted lines, make creases and unfold them.

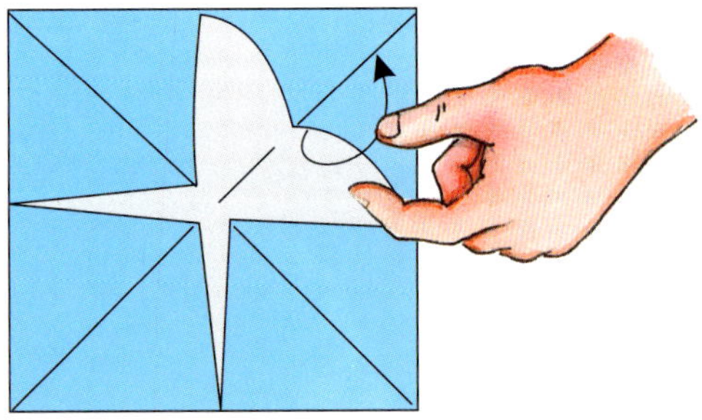

7 Insert the forefinger gently inside the pocket and lift the flap outside.

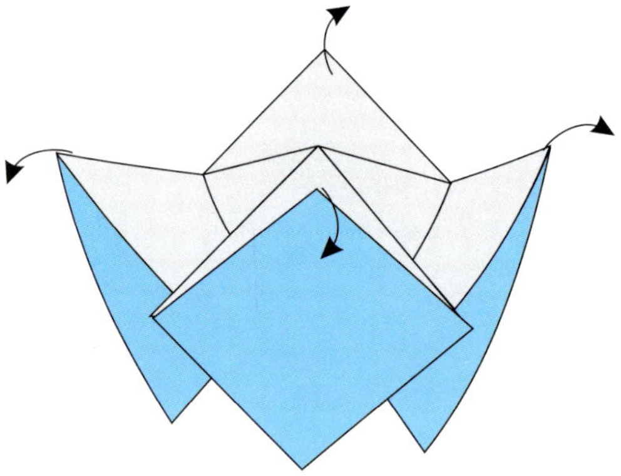

8 Open all the four flaps outwards so that the centre of the form pops up automatically.

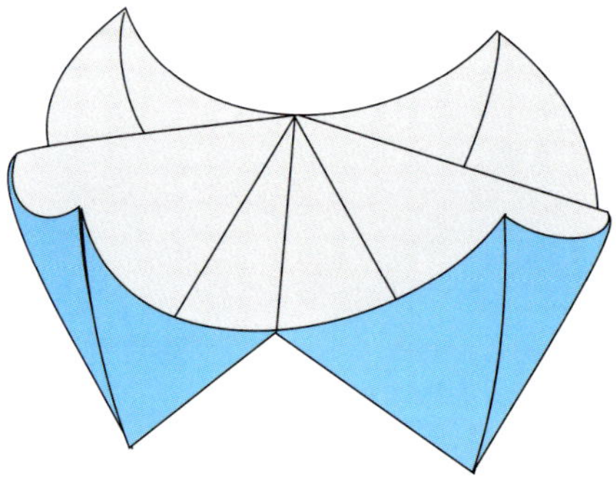

9 Your candy box is ready.

Collage Work

Tortoise

TIPS AND TRICKS

Step-1 Collect paper sheets of various colours of your own choice. Tear them in small pieces of different shapes.

Step-2 Set them within the outline and paste in the given shape.

Cut and Paste

Santa Claus

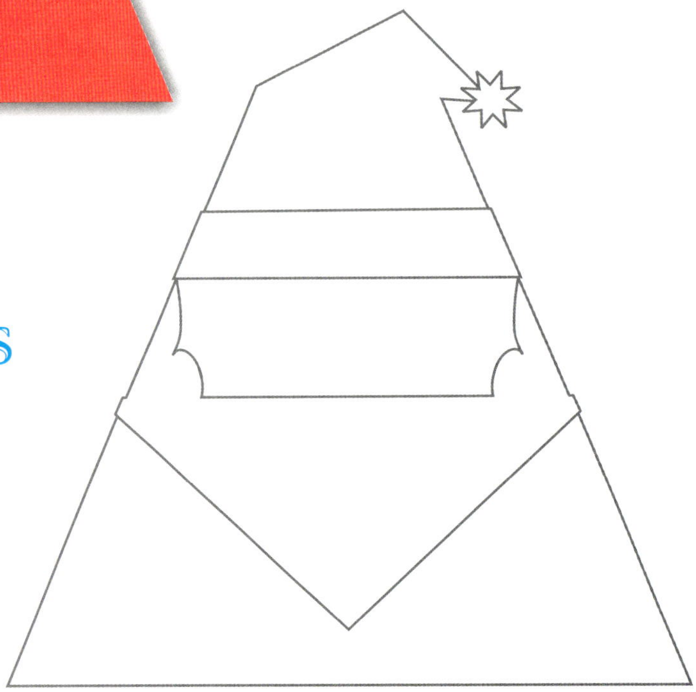

TIPS AND TRICKS

Step-1 Take craft paper sheets of various colours. Trace different parts on the shape of different colours.

Step-2 Now paste these pieces at the appropriate places.

Crushed Paper Art

Gold Fish

TIPS AND TRICKS

Step-1 Take a plain paper and squeeze it in your hand. Open it gently and apply the poster colour with a flat brush.

Step-2 Now cut the paper according to the shape and paste it within the outline.

Spray Paint

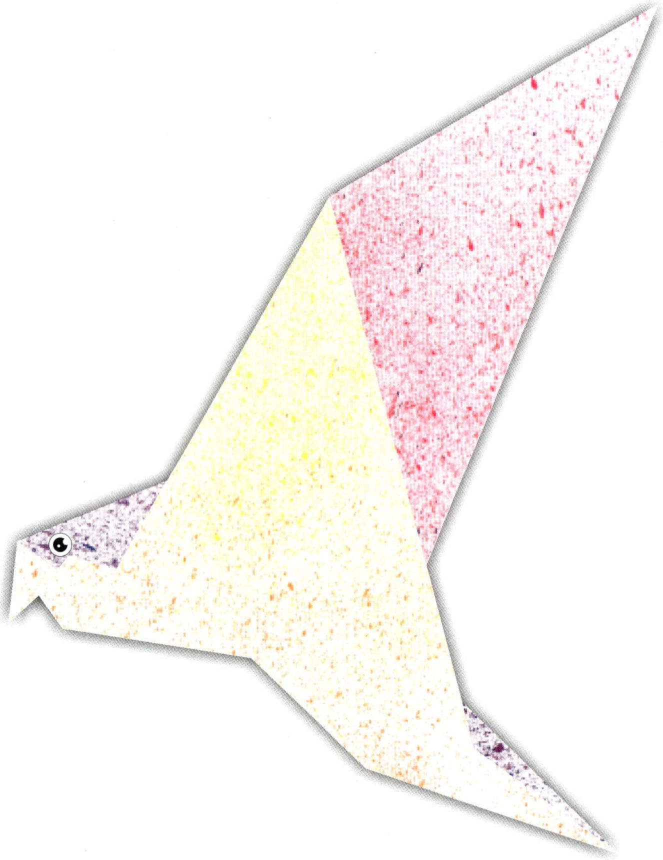

TIPS AND TRICKS

Step-1
Take a white paper. Spray different colours of your own choice with a tooth brush on the white paper.

Step-2
Cut the parts of the shape as per your liking and paste them on the figure.

Pigeon

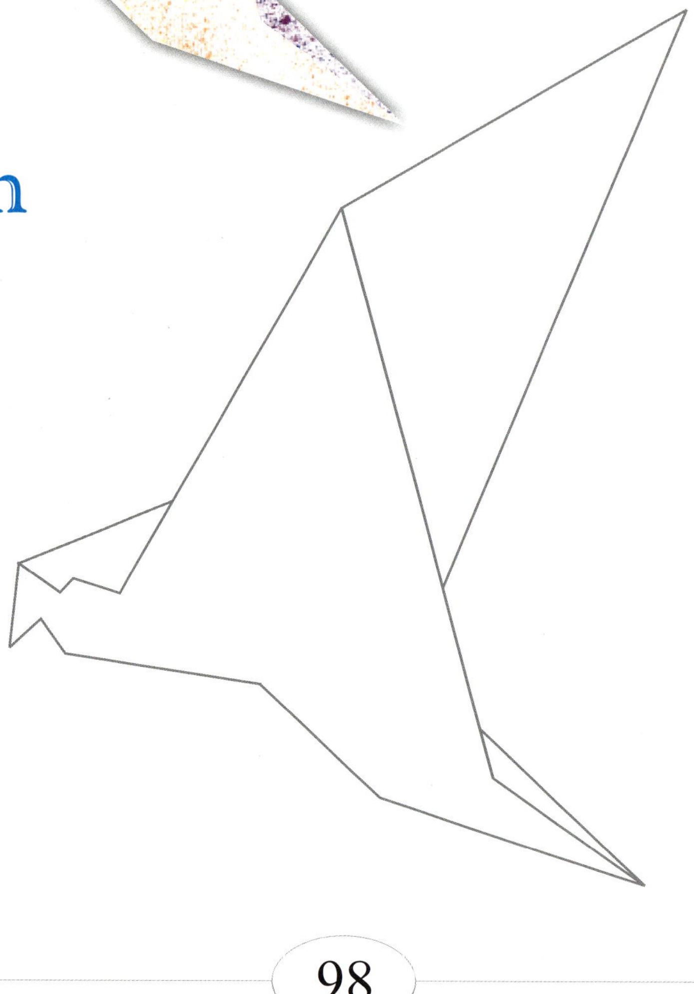

Bird-shaped Box

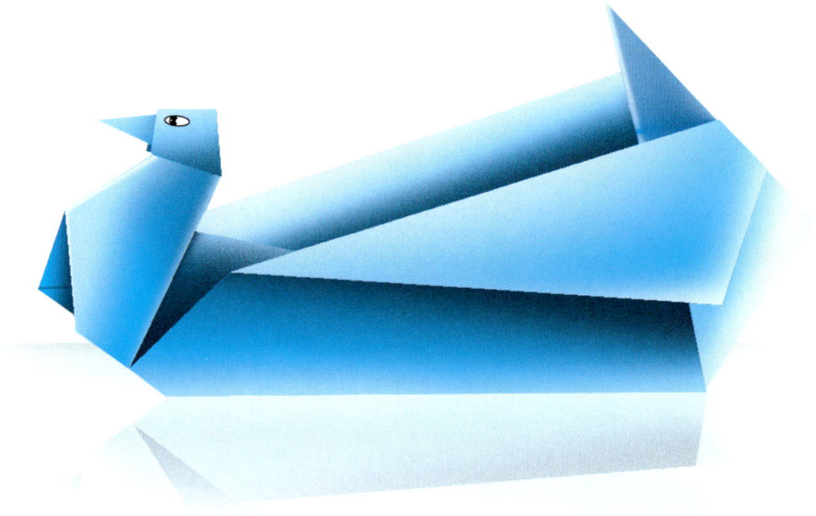

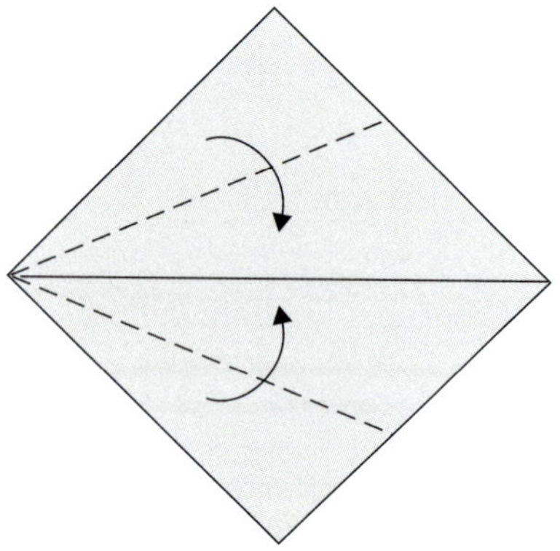

1 Make a centre crease and fold along the dotted lines.

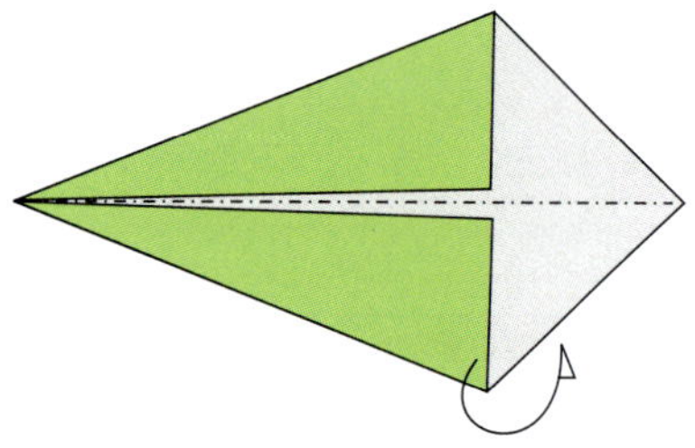

2 Make a mountain fold along the dotted line.

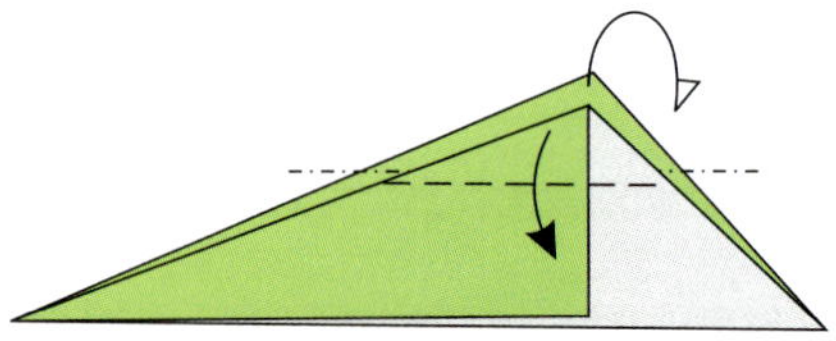

3 Fold both the top corners outwardly along the dotted lines.

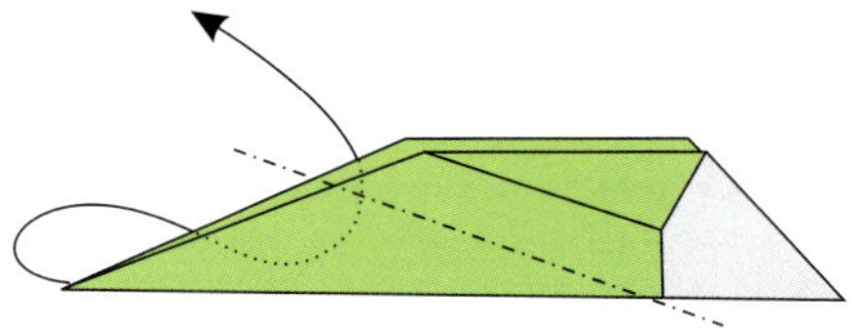

4 Make a pocket fold along the dotted line.

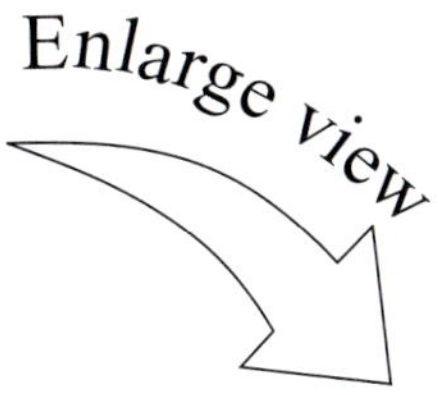

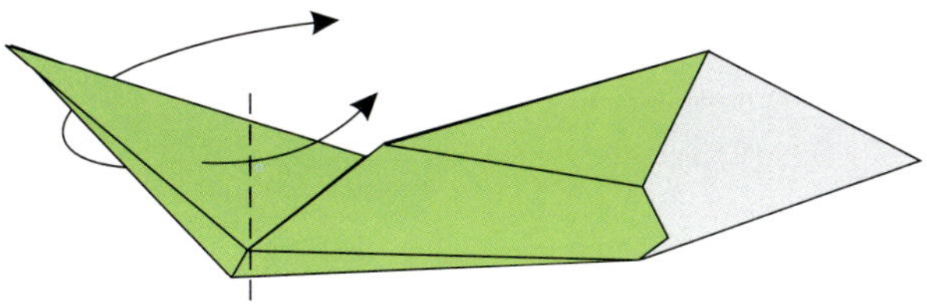

5 Again make a hood fold upside.

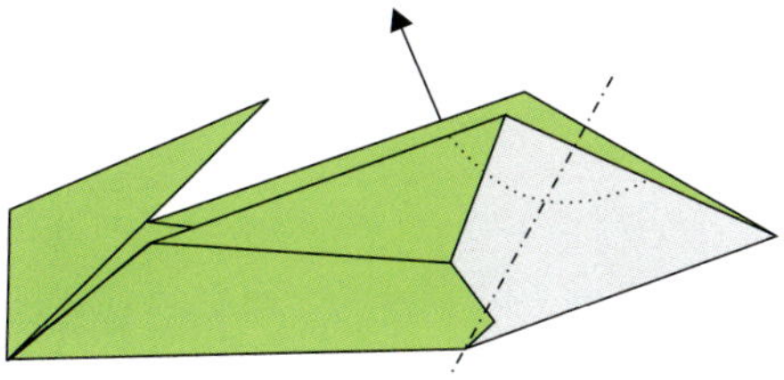

6 Make a pocket fold inside the form in the direction of the arrow.

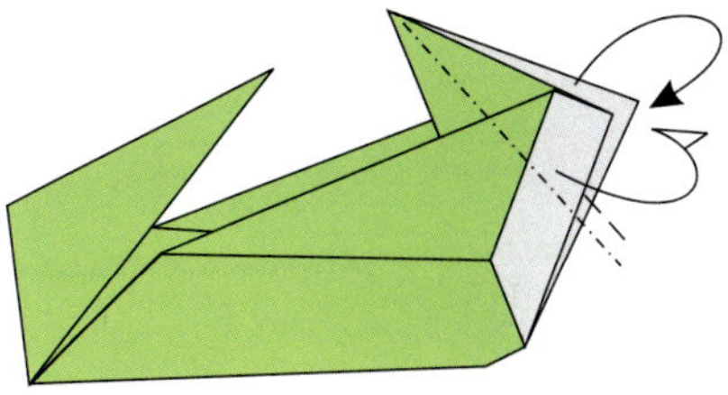

7 Fold both the flaps inside.

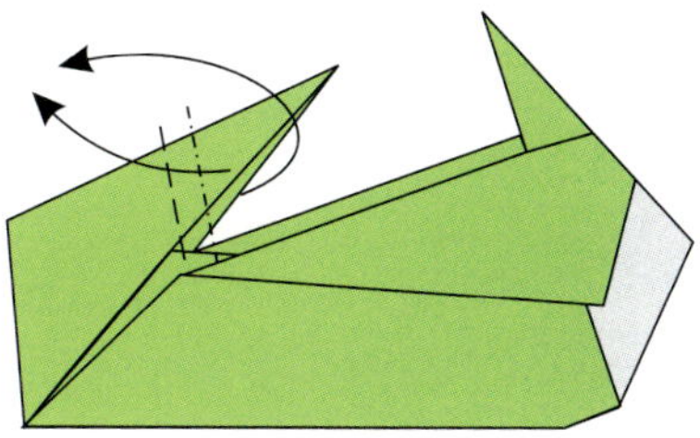

8 Again make a hood fold in the direction of arrow.

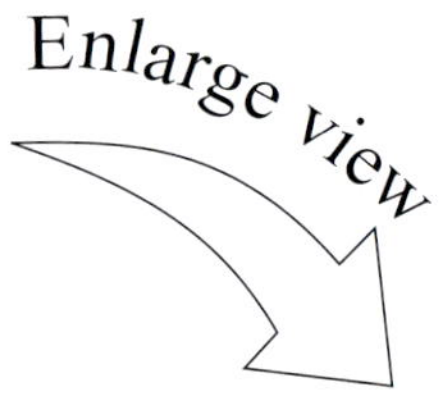

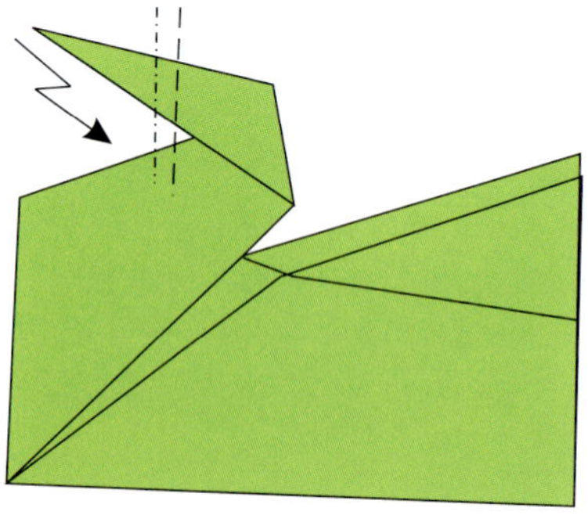

9 Make a stair-step fold for the beak.

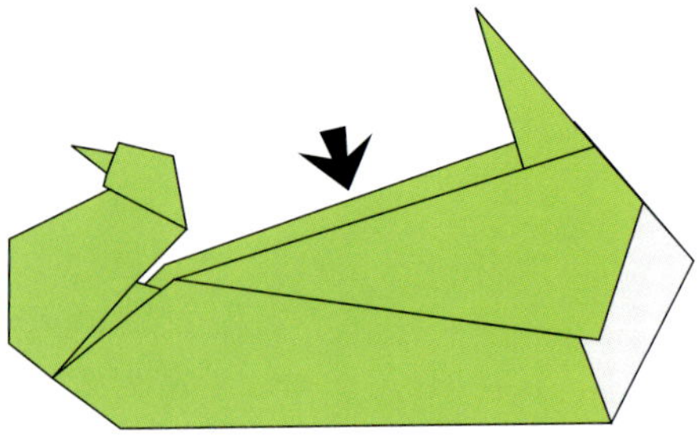

11 Open the back of the form.

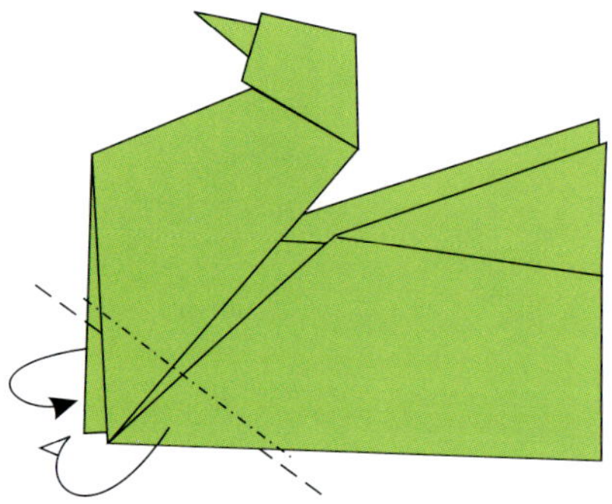

10 Fold both the corners inside as shown along the dotted lines.

12 Draw the eyes and, your bird shaped box is ready.

Monkey

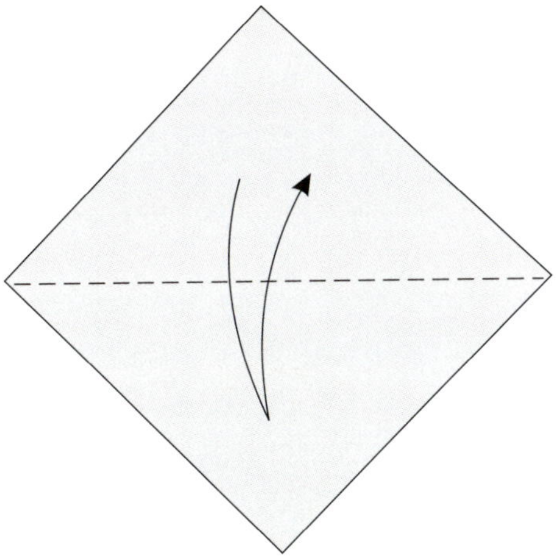

1 Fold in half to make centre crease then unfold.

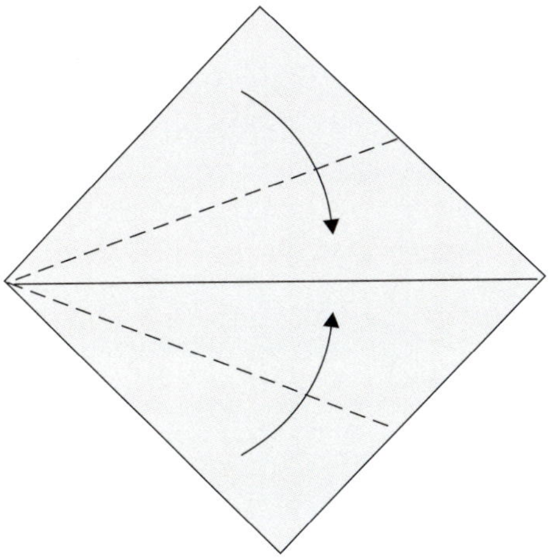

2 Fold inside along the dotted lines.

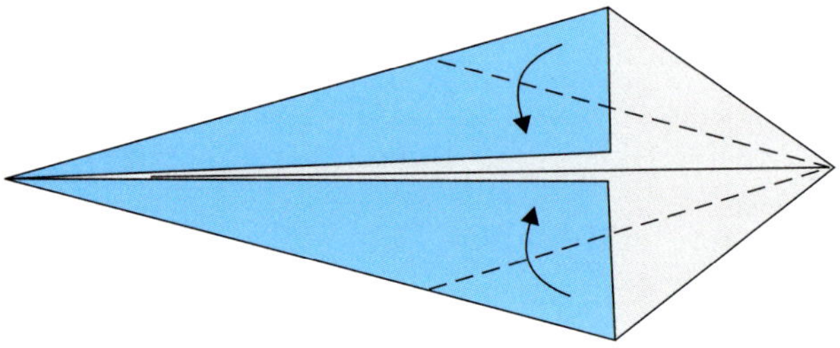

3 Again fold inside along the dotted lines.

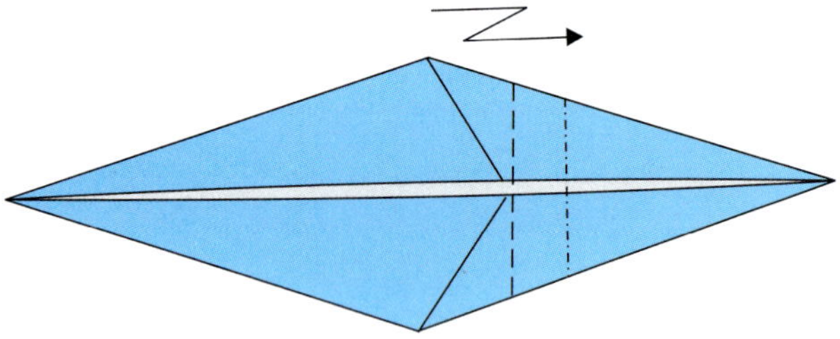

4 Make a stair-step fold along the dotted lines.

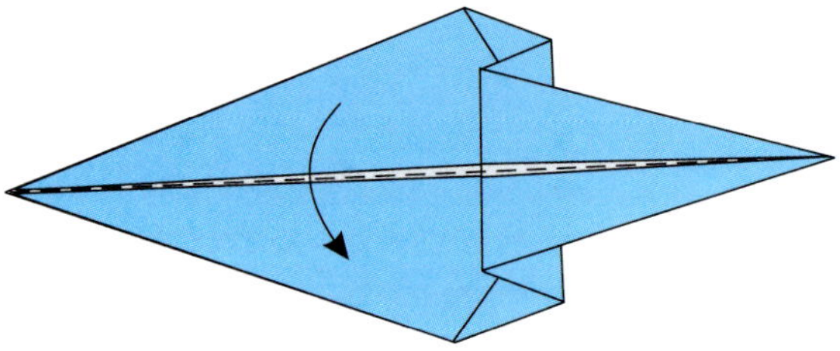

5 Fold the form in half along the dotted line.

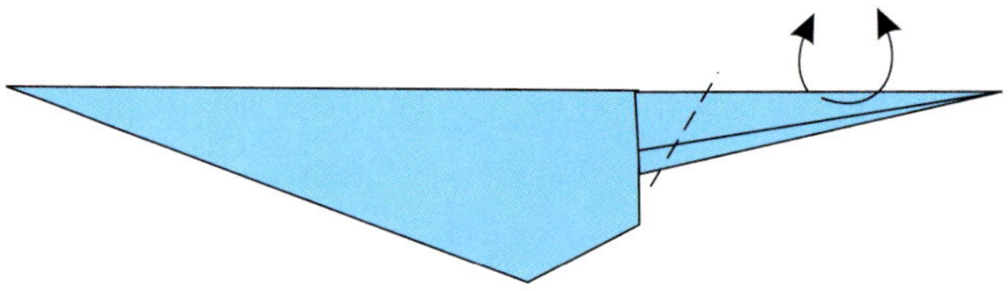

6 Now make a hood fold along the dotted line upward.

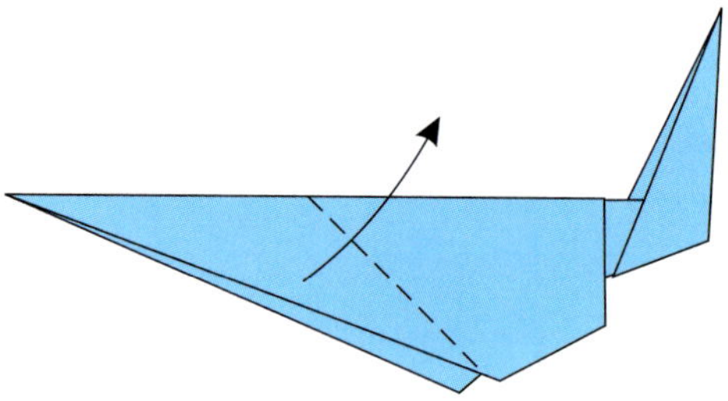

7 Make an upward fold in the direction of arrow.

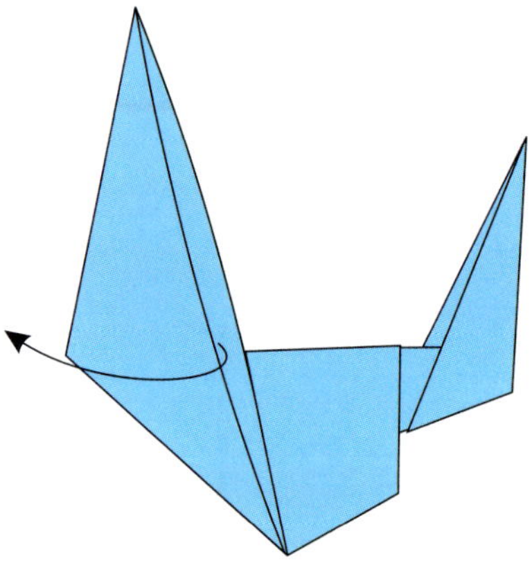

8 Now open the triangular flap by inserting your finger as shown.

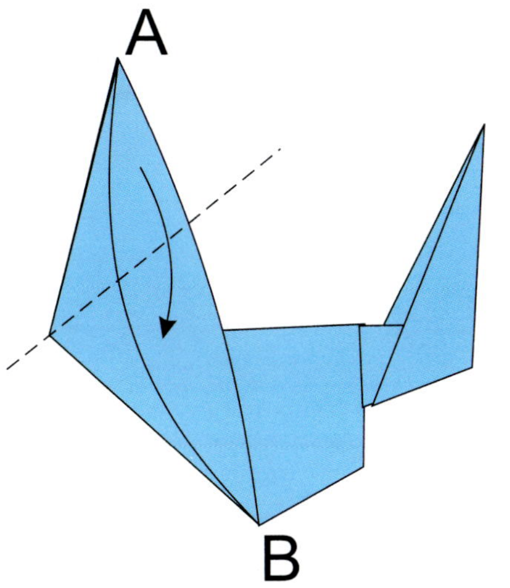

9 Fold the point ‘A’ downwards along the dotted line to meet point ‘B’....

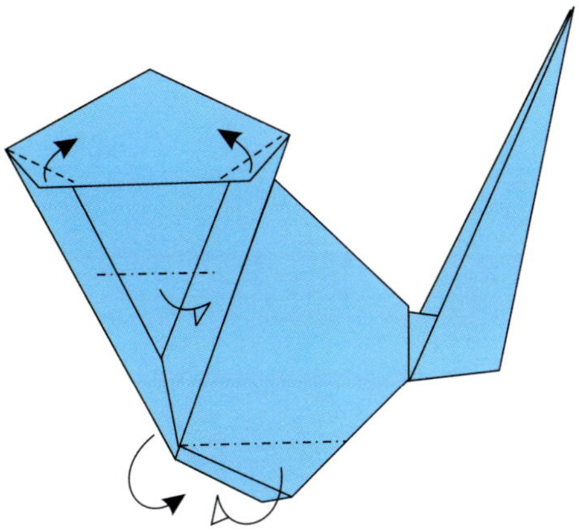

11 Fold all the flaps along the dotted lines in the direction of arrows, as shown.

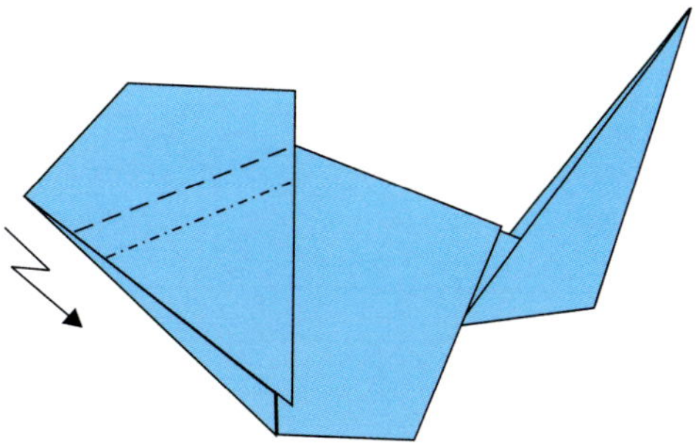

10 Make a stair-step fold on the front flap as shown.

12 Draw eyes, nose, mouth, etc, and your monkey is ready.

Giraffe

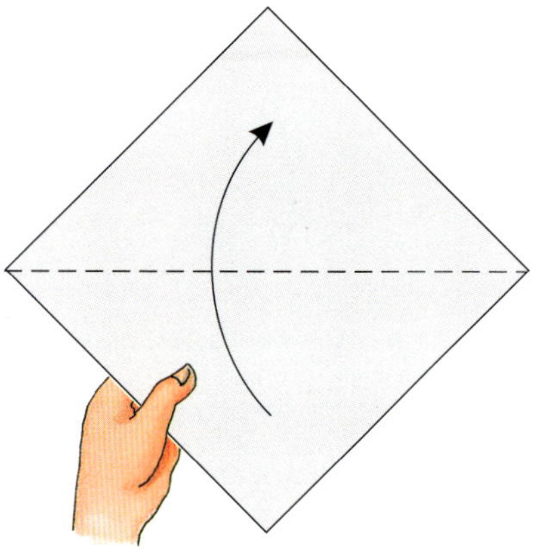

1 Fold the paper upward.

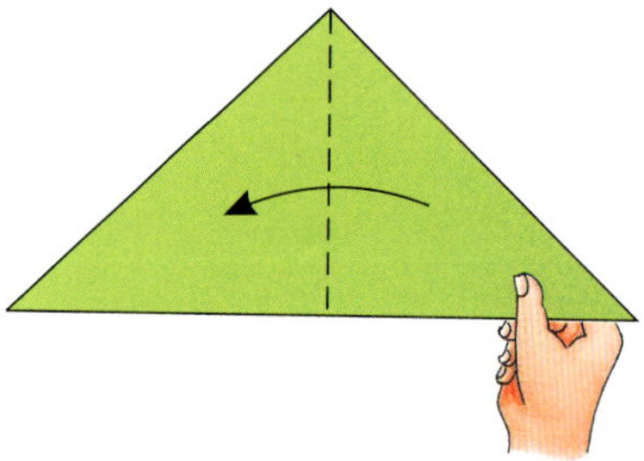

2 Fold in half along the dotted line.

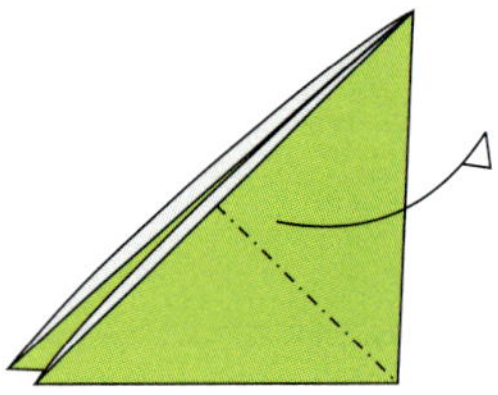

3 Put your finger inside the triangle, lift and flatten to form square on top...

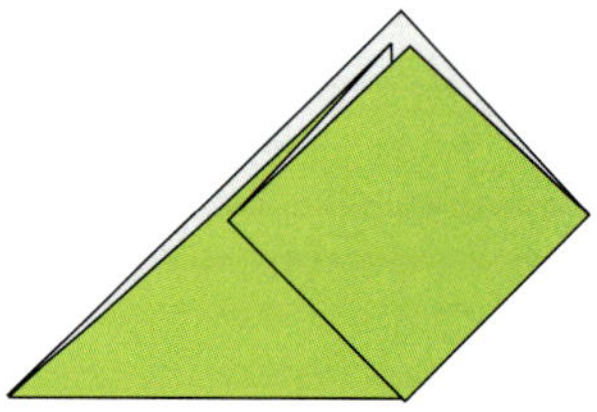

4 ....like this. Do the same with back flap also.

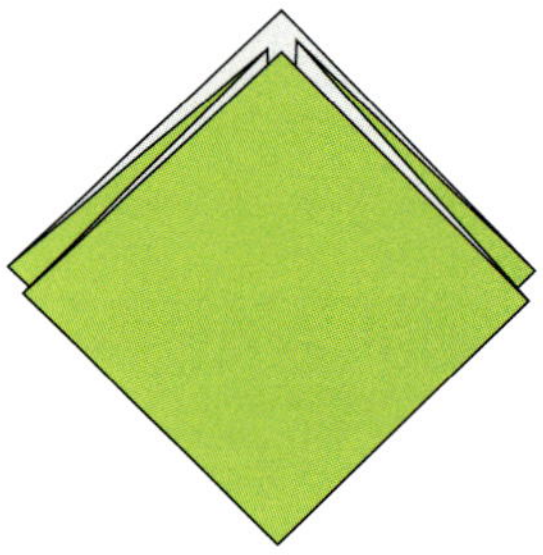

5 Your form will look like this.

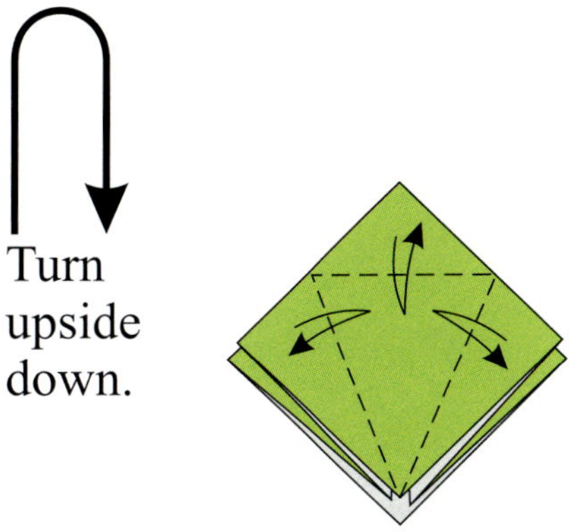

6 Make folds forward and backward along all the dotted lines and unfold them.

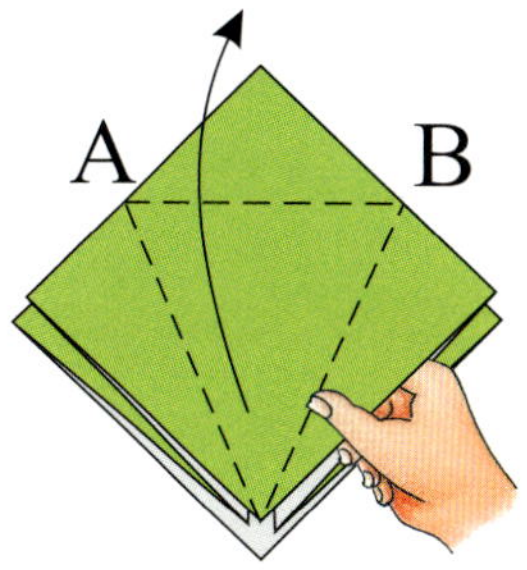

7 Pull the top flap upward by pressing along the dotted line 'AB'....

8 ....pull upward gently....

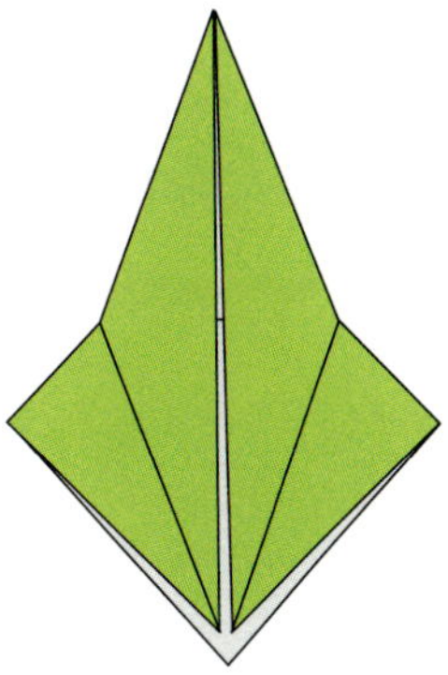

9 ....like this. Now do the same with the back flap also.

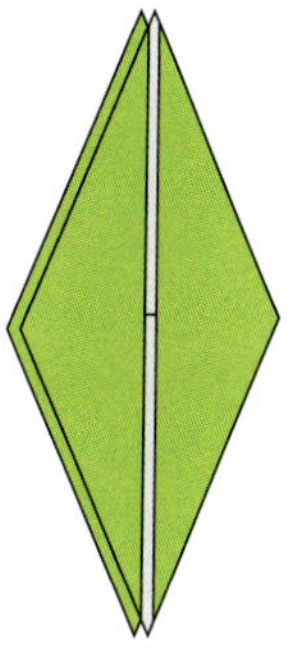

10 Your form will look like this. Now open the whole paper.

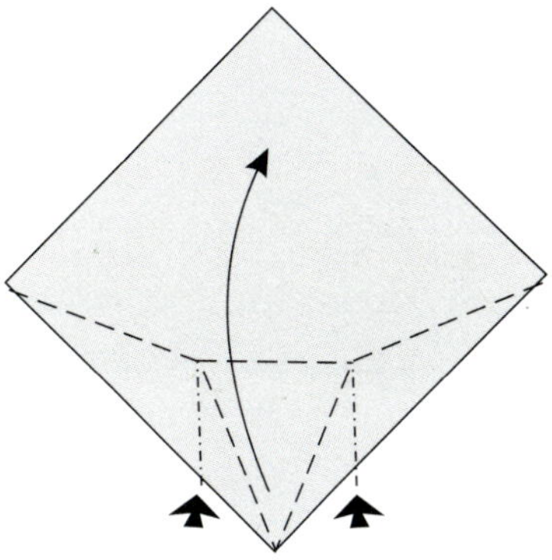

11 Fold bottom triangle up over centre, along the dotted lines and press the right and left sides.

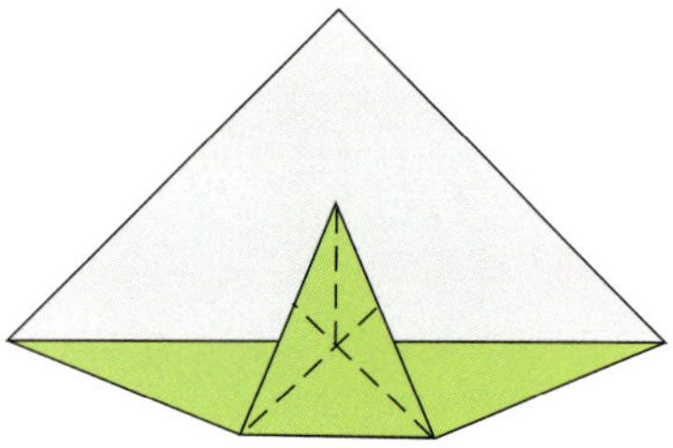

12 After folding in this manner, fold and unfold along all the three dotted lines as shown.

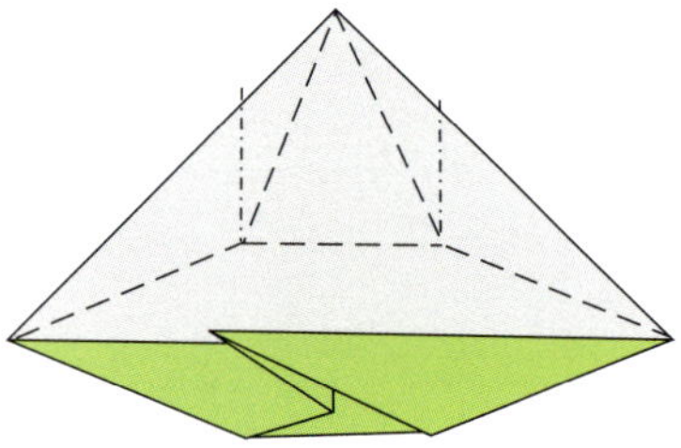

13 Repeat the same steps no. 11 and 12 with the upper flap.

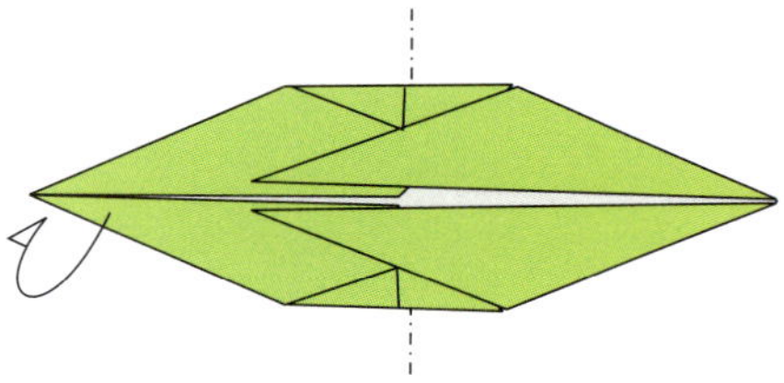

14 Your form will look like this. Now fold left side backward along the dotted line and bring the right corner vertically upside.

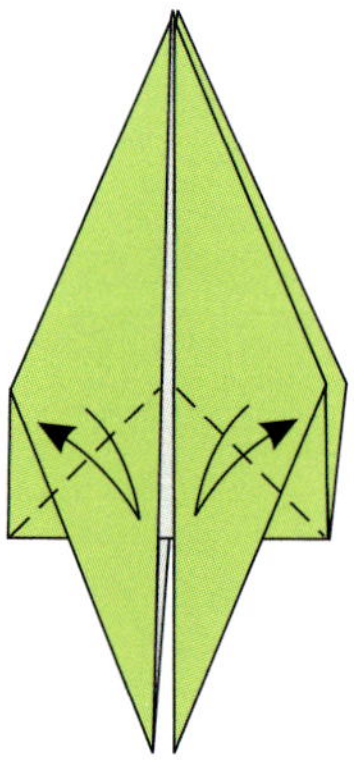

15 Fold and unfold the bottom flaps along the dotted lines.

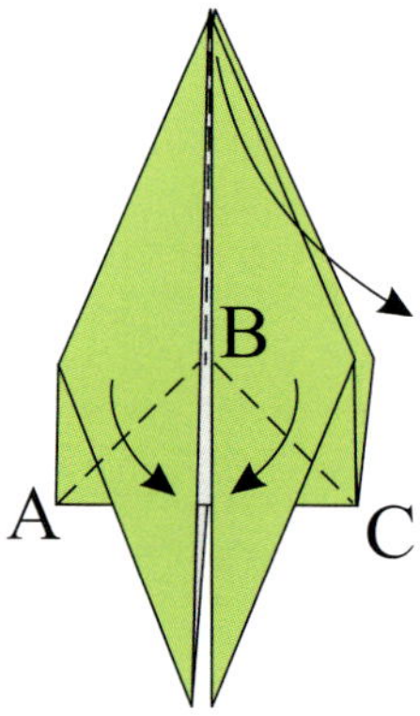

16 Now fold along the dotted lines 'AB' and 'BC' so the point 'A' and 'C' meet each other. On doing this the top flap will stood upright.

17 Fold the standing flap to right side. Your form will look like this.

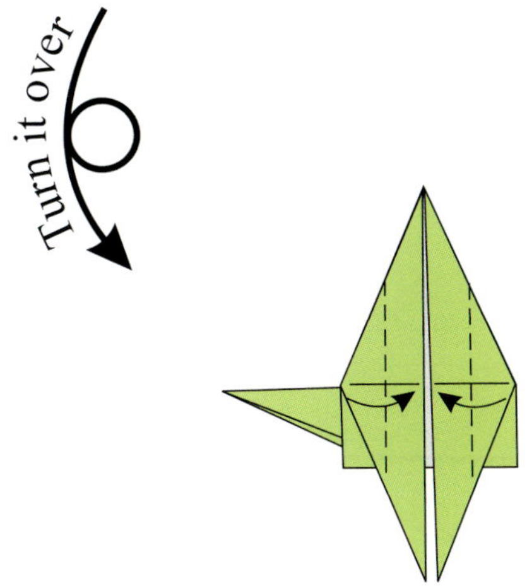

18 Fold both the sides inwards along the dotted lines.

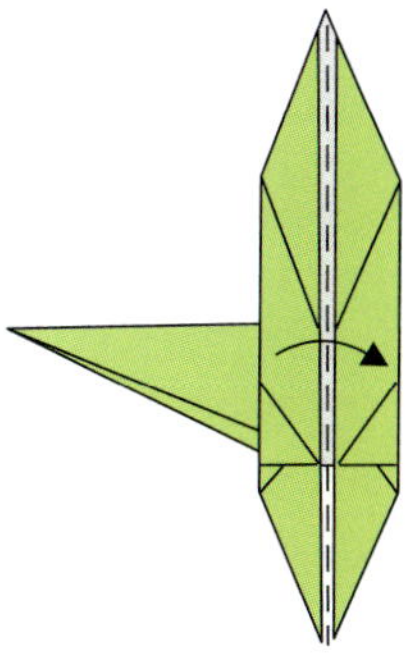

19 Now fold the form in half so that the left side will overlap the right side.

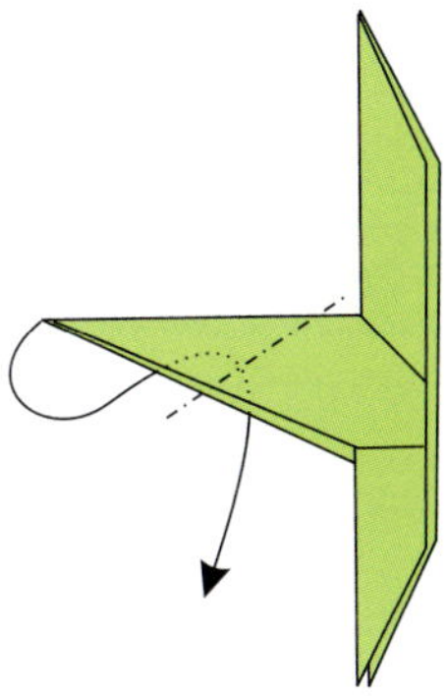

20 Fold inward along the dotted line to make a pocket fold.

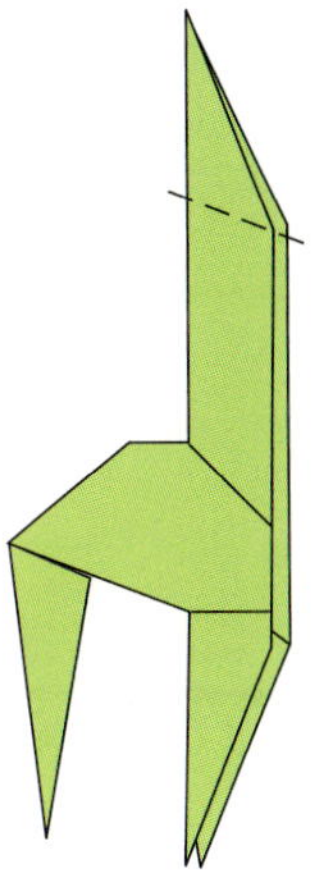

21 Make a hood fold along the dotted line.

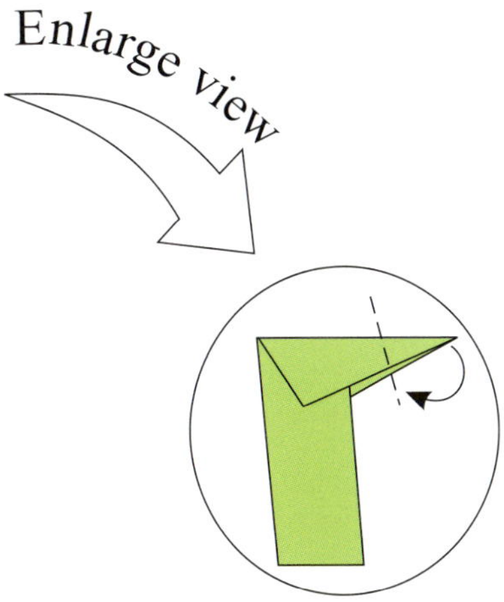

22 Fold the corner inside.

23 Decorate your giraffe and draw the eyes.

Flower

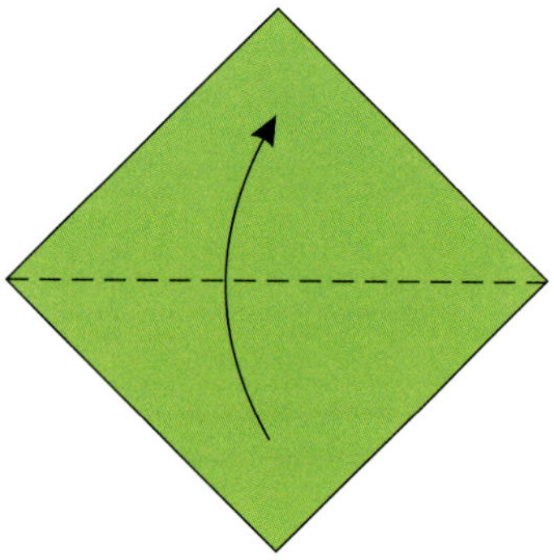

1 Fold in half.

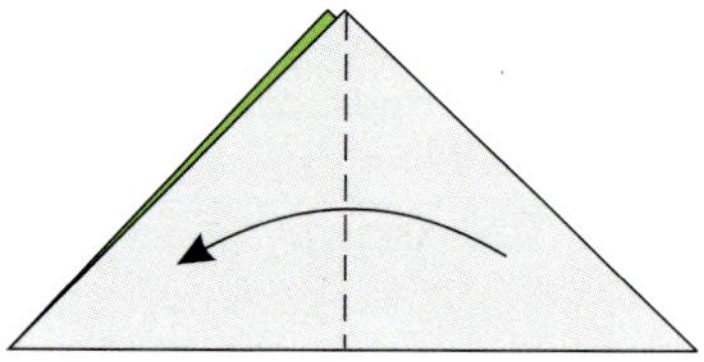

2 Again fold in half.

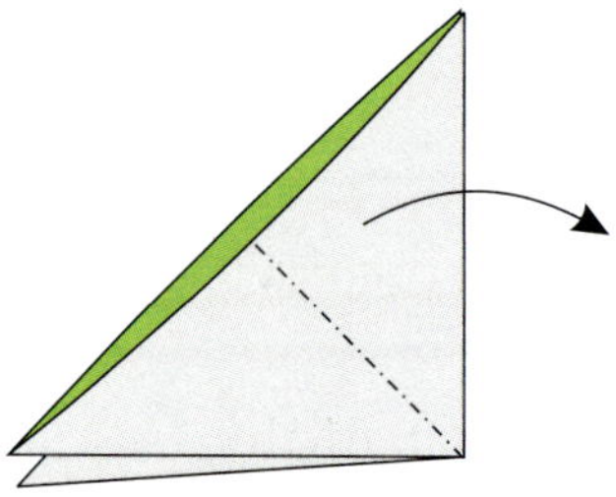

3 Put your finger inside the upper triangle and lift. Flatten to form square on top.

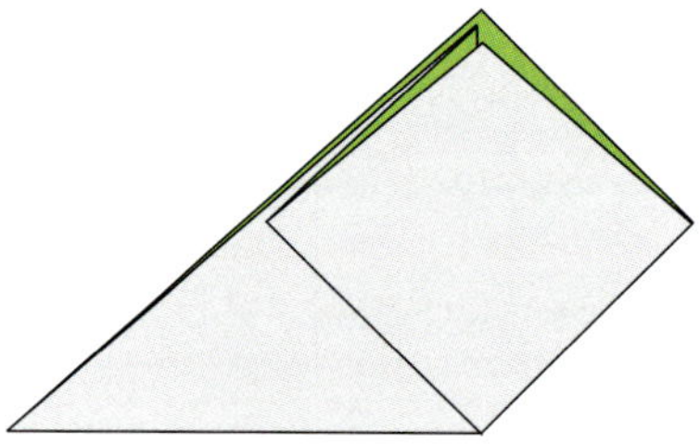

4 Fold the backside in the same way.

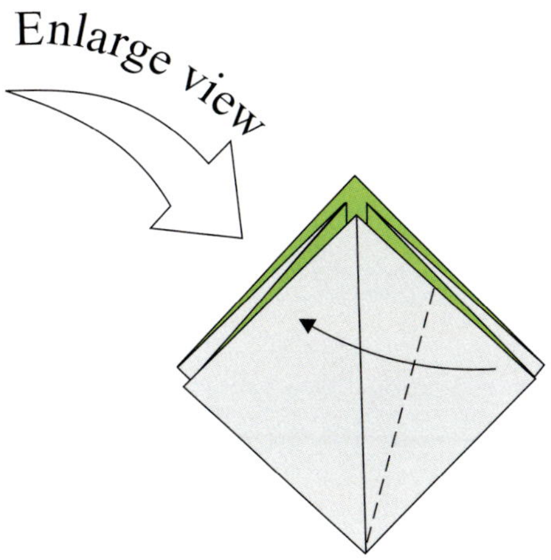

5 Fold inwards as shown.

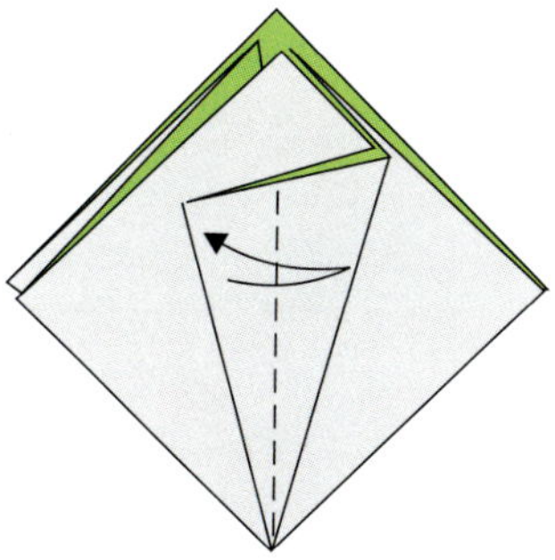

6 Fold and unfold, then put your finger inside, lift and flatten.

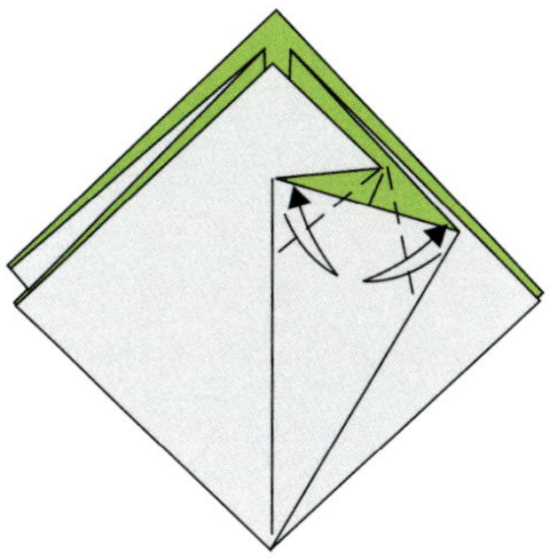

7 Now fold and unfold as shown.

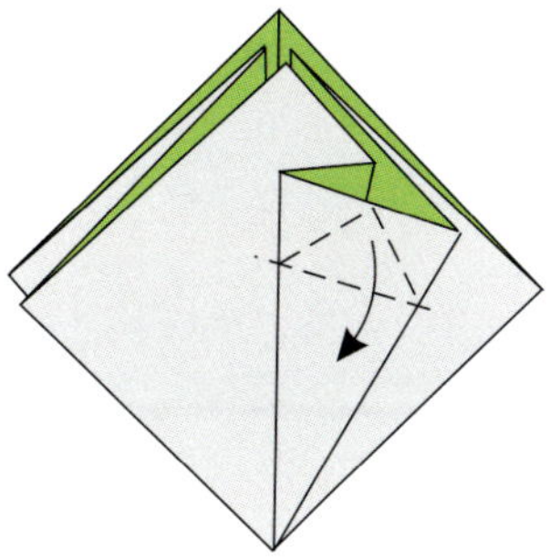

8 Fold downward....

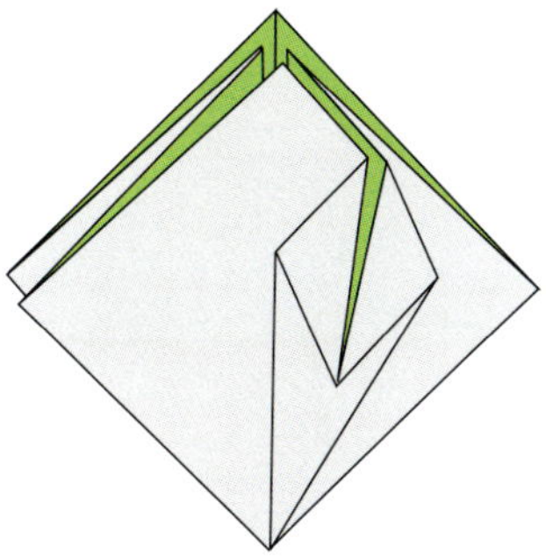

9 ....like this. Now do the same with the other three sides.

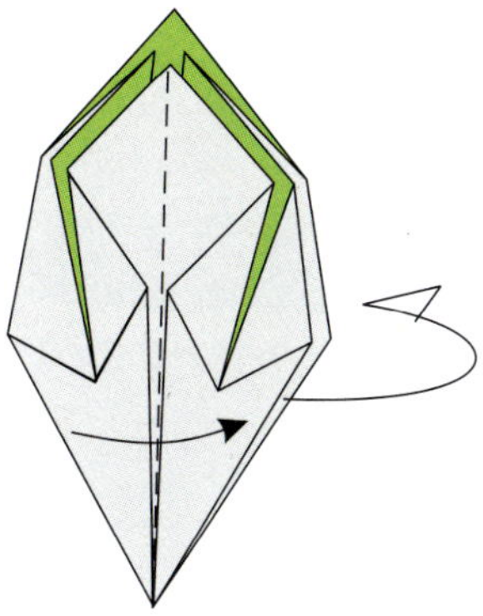

10 Fold the upper layer in half and do the same with the back layer.

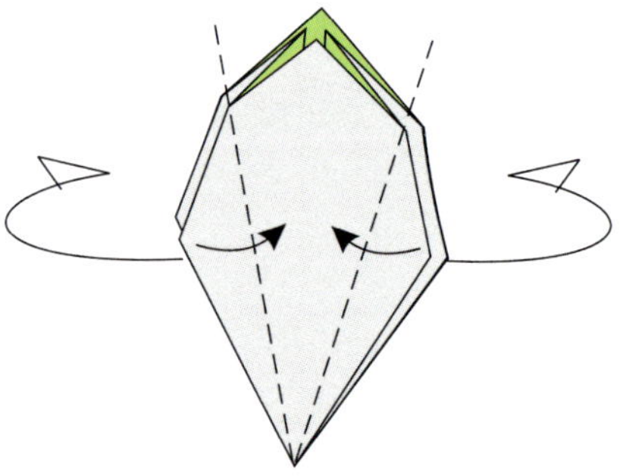

11 Fold as shown. Make same folds at the backside also.

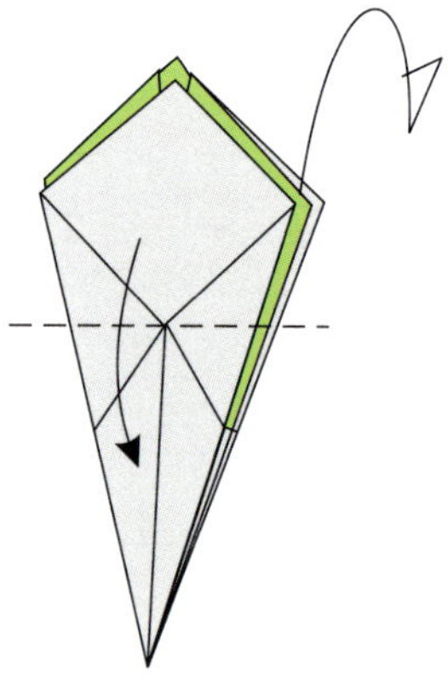

12 Make downward fold. Make same fold at the backside also.

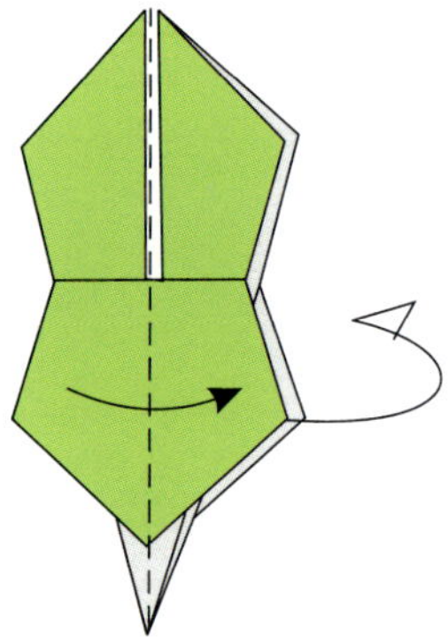

13 Fold in half. Make same fold at the backside also.

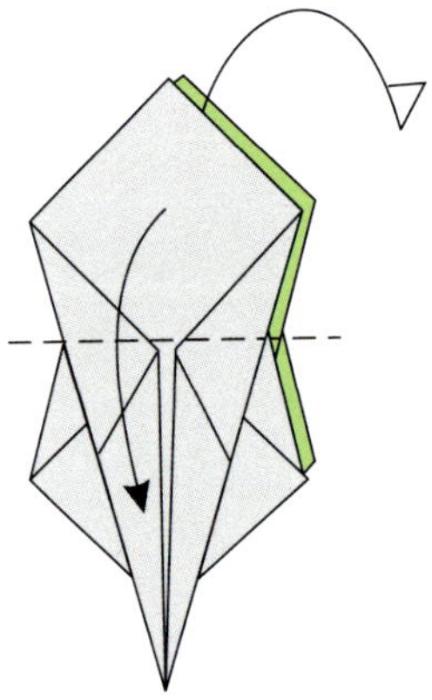

14 Fold in half. Make same fold at the backside also.

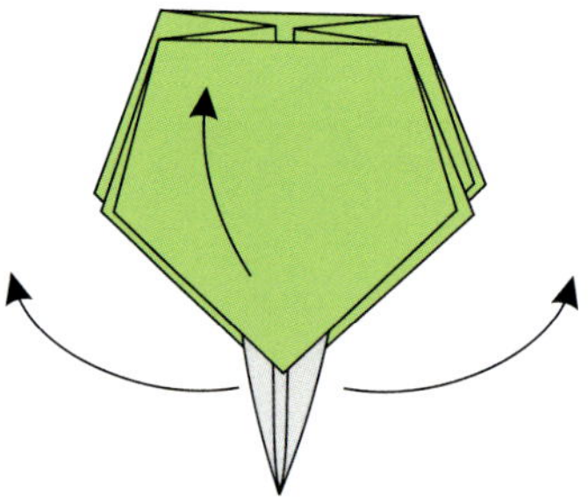

15 Now open all the four flaps so as to make the petals of the flower.

16 Flower is ready.

Crab

1 Fold the paper along the dotted lines and unfold it.

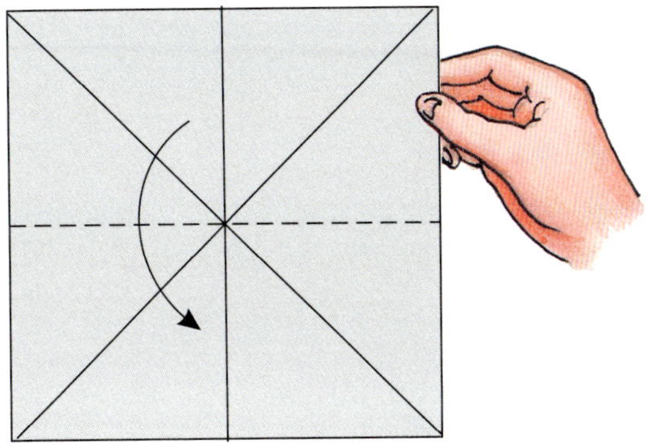

2 Fold along the dotted line.

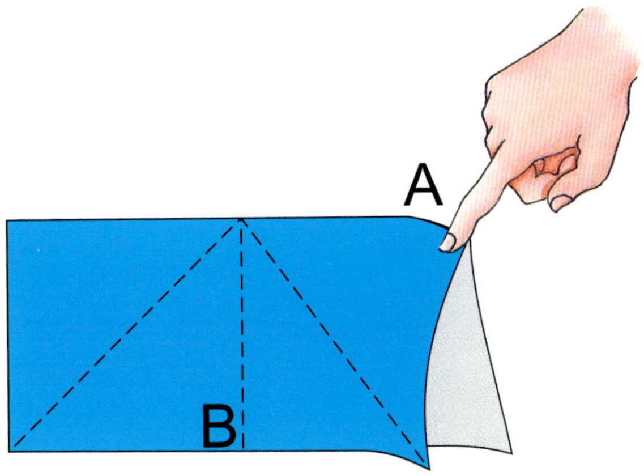

3 Push right side down at the point 'A' inside of the form to meet point 'B'.

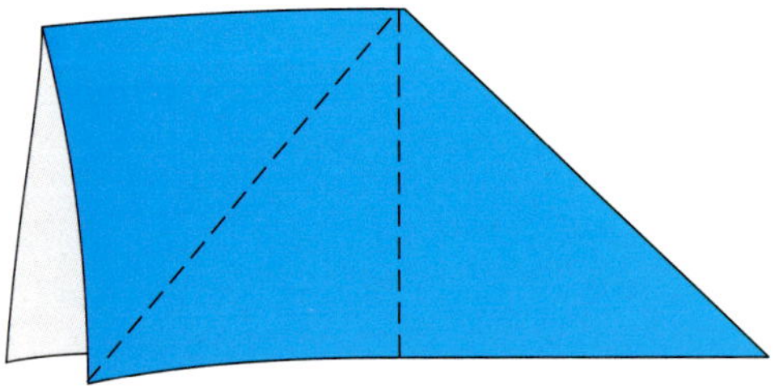

4 Repeat the previous step with the left side also.

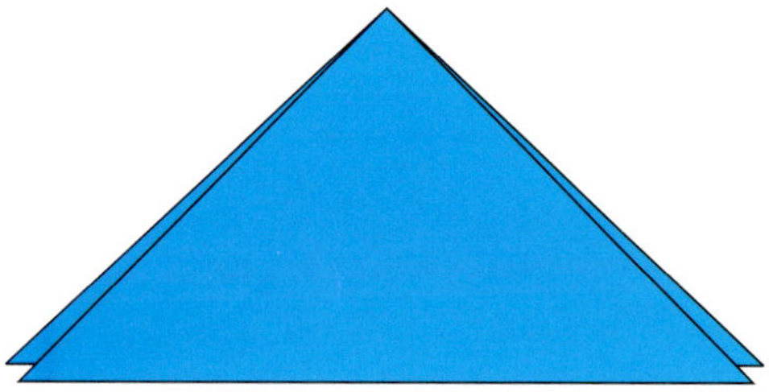

5 Your form will now look like this.

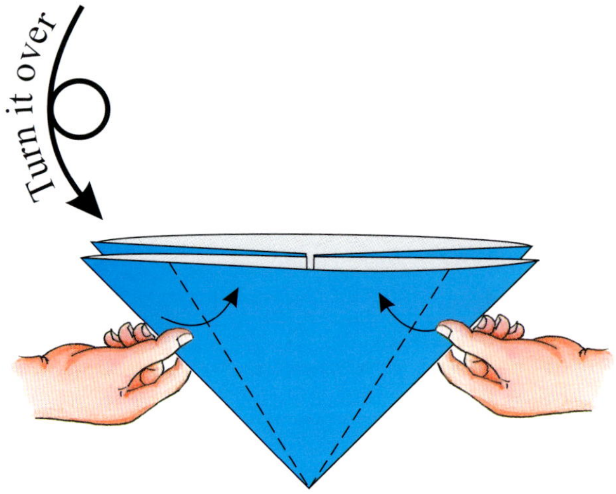

6 Fold the sides of the upper layer as shown.

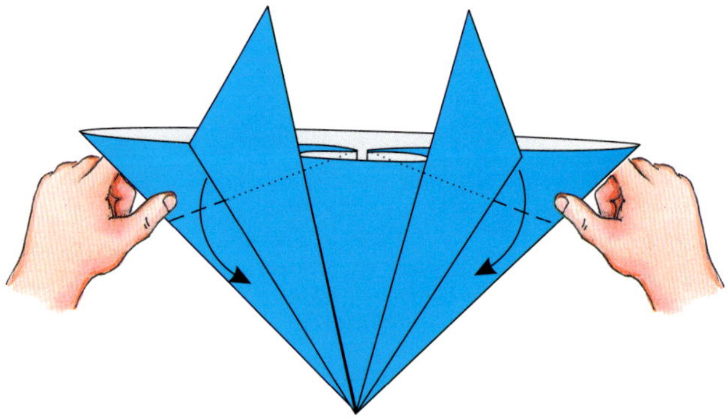

7 Fold down the flaps of the lower layer downwards....

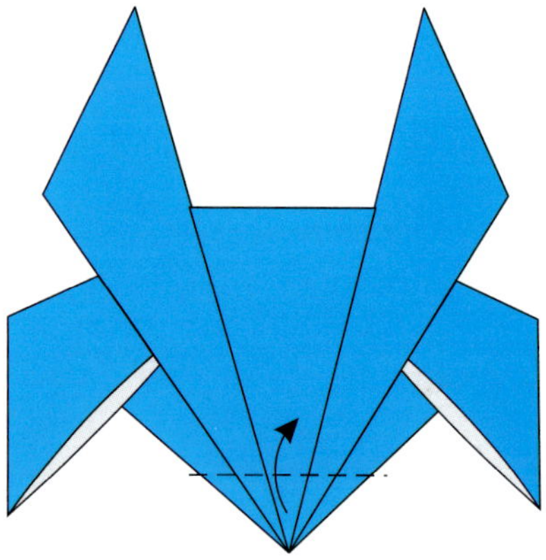

8 .... like this, and fold the lower tip upwards along the dotted line.

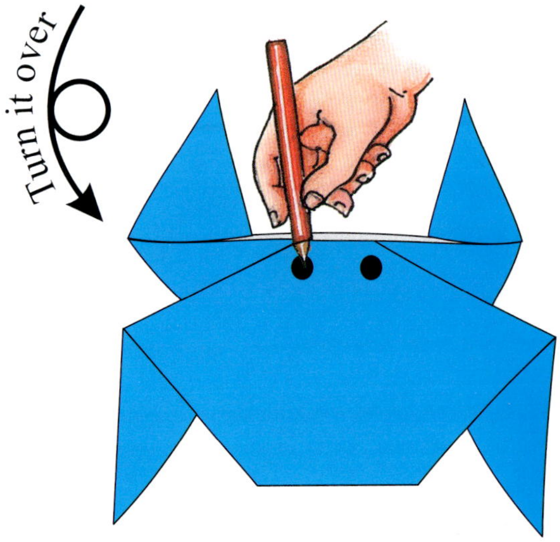

9 Draw eyes of the crab.

Rabbit

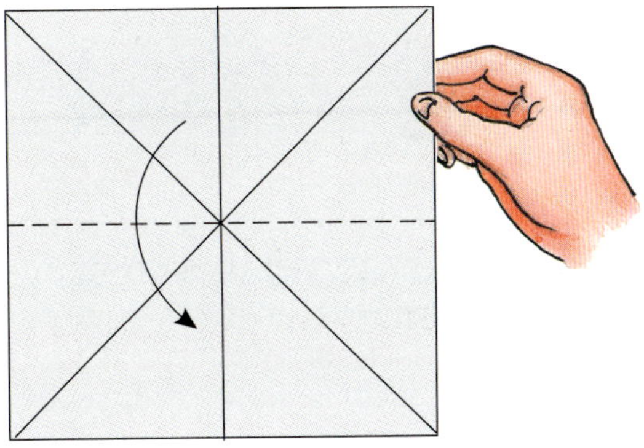

2 Fold along the dotted line.

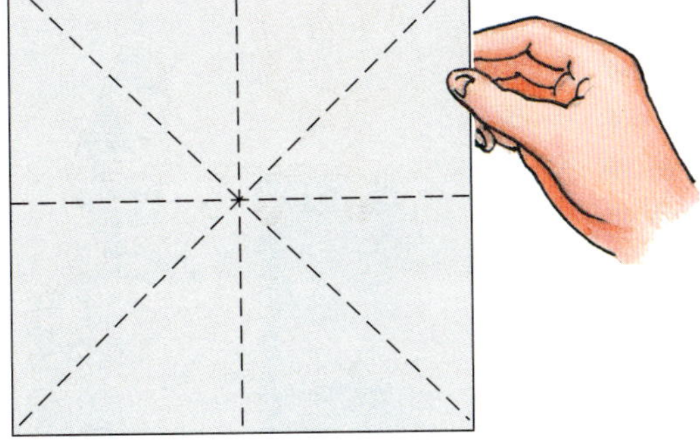

1 Fold the paper along the dotted lines and unfold it.

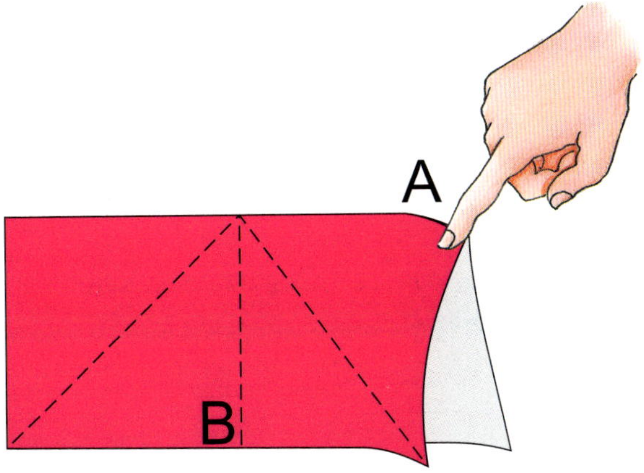

3 Push right side at the point 'A' down inside of the form to meet point 'B'.

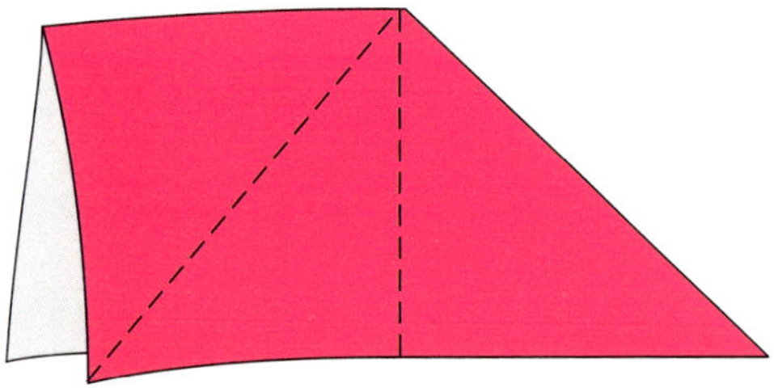

4 Repeat the previous step with the left side also.

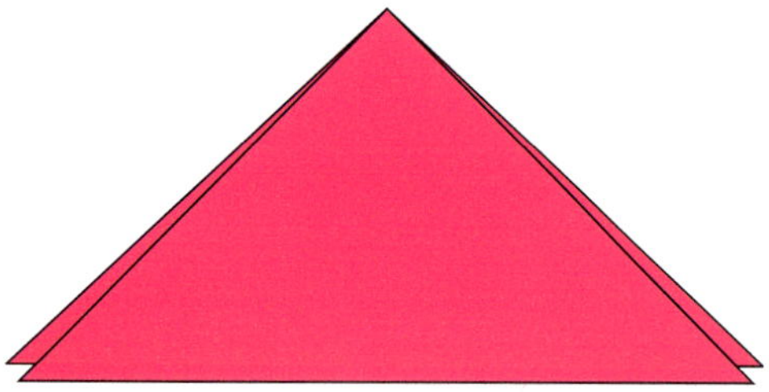

5 Your form will now look like this.

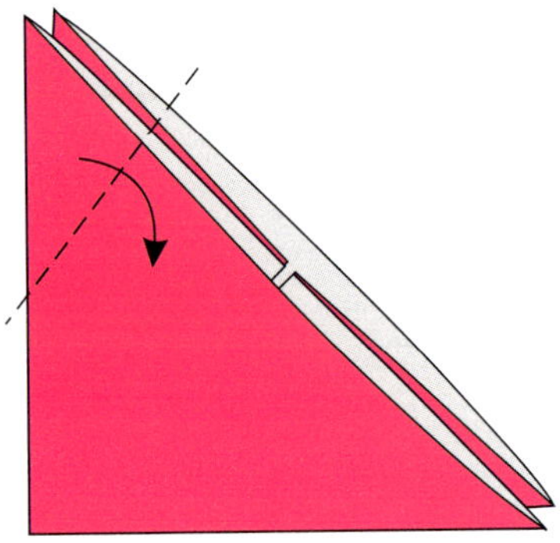

6 Put the form in this manner and use the valley fold to fold the top corner along the dotted line....

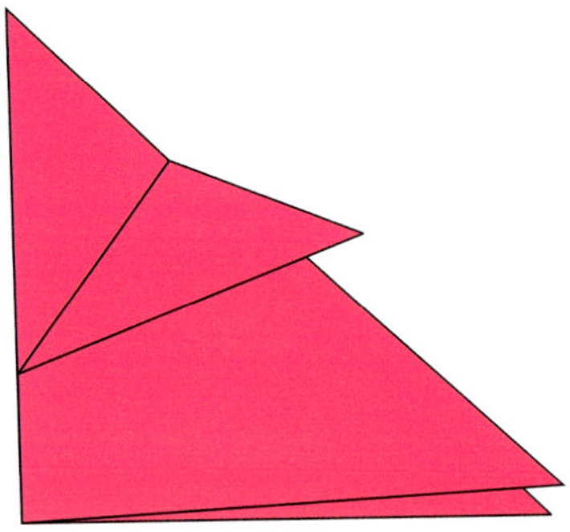

7 ...like this.

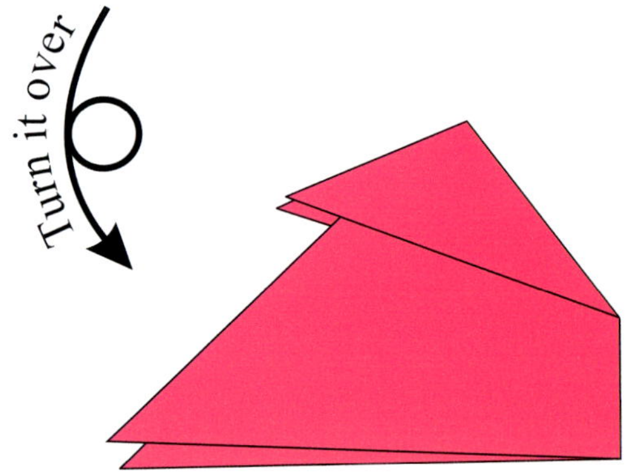

8 Repeat the same step with other side.

9 Draw eyes, legs and whiskers. To add a fuzzy tail, paste a cotton ball on the two outer sides

Collage Work

Crab

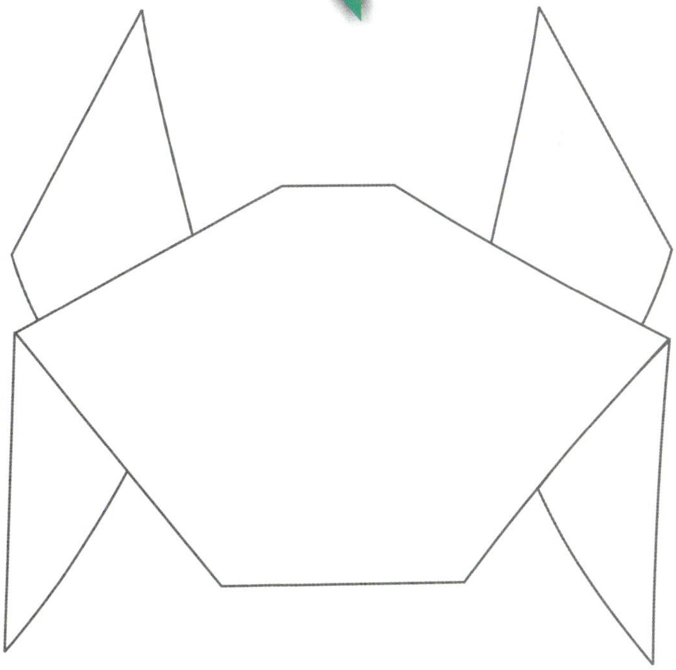

TIPS AND TRICKS

Step-1 Collect paper sheets of various colours of your own choice. Tear them in small pieces of different shapes.

Step-2 Set them within the outline and paste in the given shape.

Cut and Paste

Bird-Shaped Box

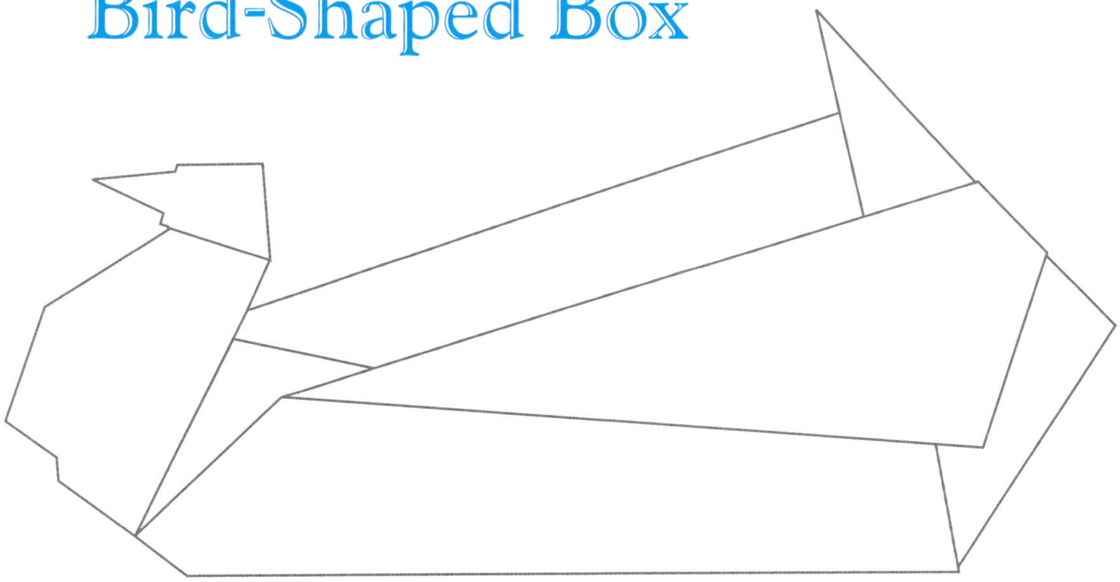

TIPS AND TRICKS

Step-1 Take craft paper sheets of various colours. Trace different parts on the shape of different colours.

Step-2 Now paste these pieces at the appropriate places.

Crushed Paper Art

TIPS AND TRICKS

Step-1 Take a plain paper and squeeze it in your hand. Open it gently and apply the poster colour with a flat brush.

Step-2 Now cut the paper according to the shape and paste it within the outline.

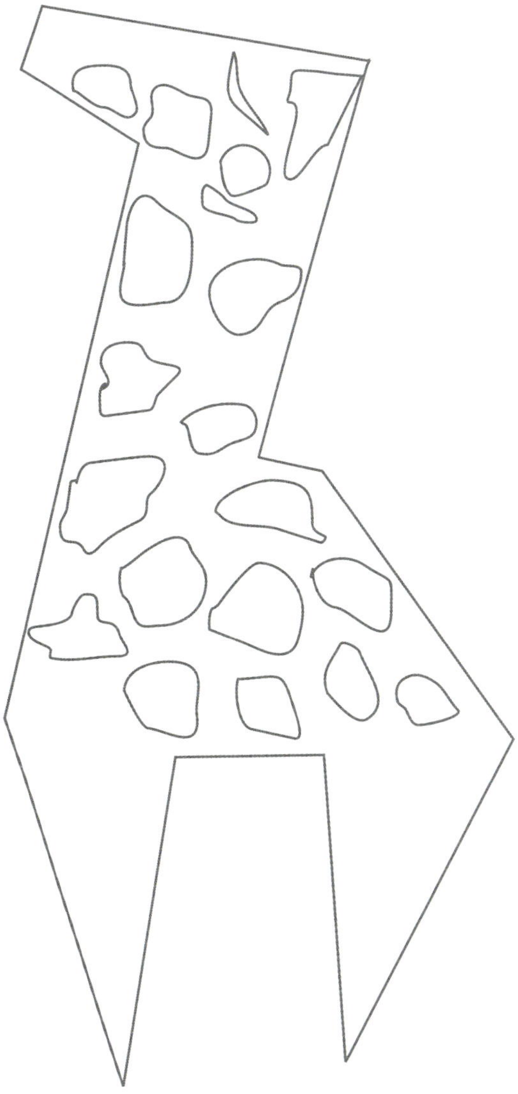

Giraffe

Spray Paint

TIPS AND TRICKS

Step-1
Take a white paper. Spray different colours of your own choice with a tooth brush on the white paper.
Step-2
Cut the parts of the shape as per your liking and paste them on the figure.

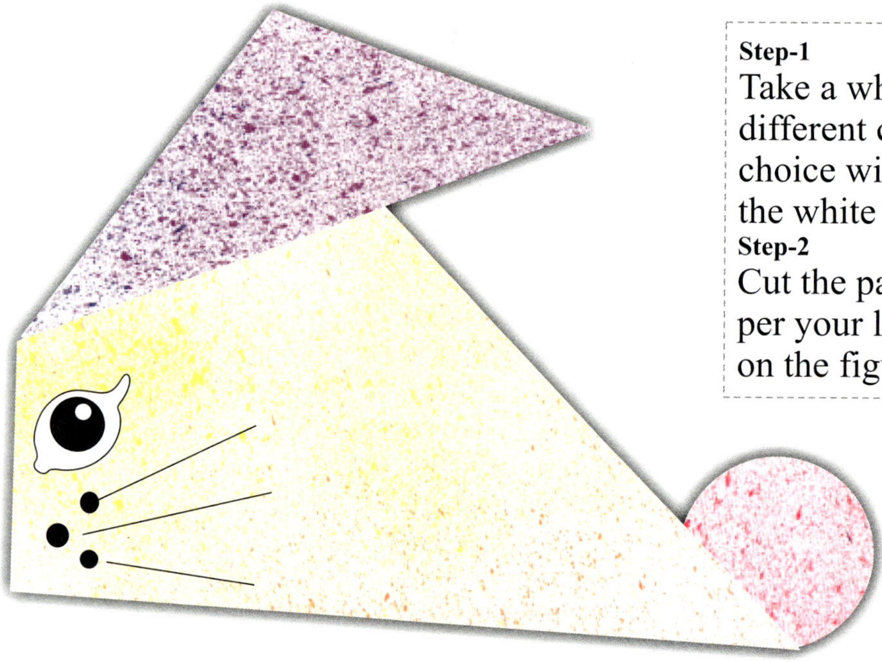

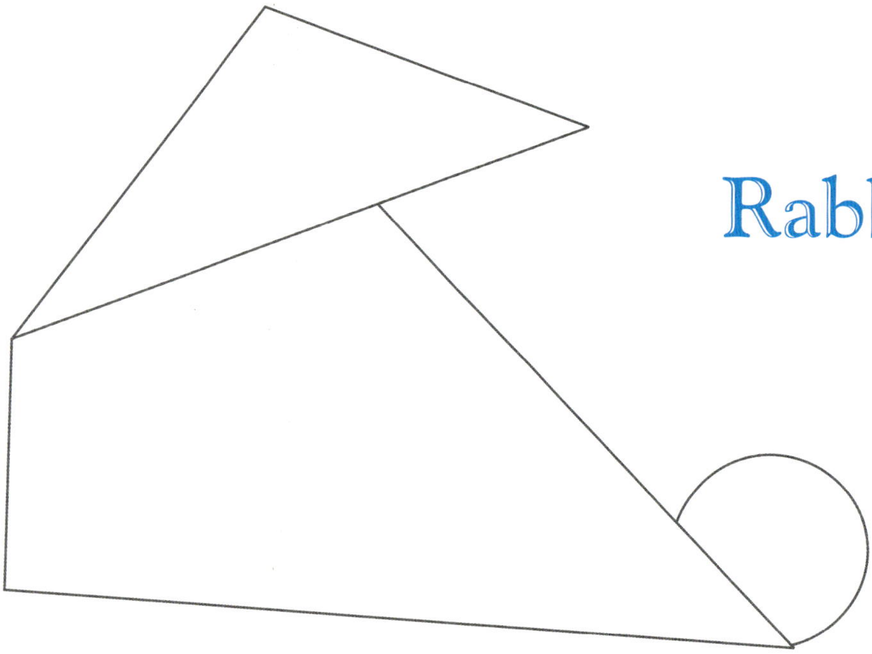

Rabbit